Gun Shot Witness

The Tim Remington Story

Amy Joy Hess

Ocean To Mountain Publishing
PO BOX 60
Mullan, ID 83846
www.otmpub.com

This book is based on the true-life experiences of Pastor Tim Remington, his family, and members of The Altar Church of Coeur d'Alene Idaho

Gun Shot Witness: The Tim Remington Story
Copyright © 2023 by Amy Joy Hess
Created in the United States by Ocean To Mountain Publishing

No part of this book may be reproduced in any manner whatsoever without written permission except in the case of brief quotations with due credit. For information, address Ocean To Mountain Publishing, P.O. Box 60, Mullan, ID 83846.

Books published by Ocean To Mountain Publishing are available at special discounts for bulk purchases in the United States by corporations, institutions, and interested individuals.

Bible quotations are from the King James Version.

Cover photographs by Sonya and Mike Siedschlag.
Cover design by Amy Joy Hess.
Photographs without attribution are the work of Amy Joy Hess.

ISBN: 978-1-962532-00-6

For God, who commanded the light to shine out of darkness, hath shined in our hearts, to give the light of the knowledge of the glory of God in the face of Jesus Christ. But we have this treasure in earthen vessels, that the excellency of the power may be of God, and not of us. We are troubled on every side, yet not distressed; we are perplexed, but not in despair; persecuted, but not forsaken; cast down, but not destroyed.

                                          2 Corinthians 4:6-9

When Jesus walked this fallen world, He proclaimed, "The kingdom of heaven is at hand," and so the lame walked, the blind could see, the souls of mankind were rescued and healed. In these pages we find a taste, a sampling that the kingdom of heaven is still among us. Through these lives we see that Jesus the King is still close at hand, reaching through pain and suffering to reveal the heavenly, just as the clouds part to reveal the stars. Because Jesus is here, hope, healing, and courage are here.

-Frank Peretti
author of *This Present Darkness*
and friend to Tim Remington

Table of Contents

	Introduction	3
1.	On Fire	5
2.	Tim and Cindy	15
3.	The Family	25
4.	GSWs	33
5.	Miracles on the Edge	39
6.	Kyle Odom	45
7.	The Puzzle Ball	55
8.	Cataldo Lighthouse	59
9.	Justine	73
10.	Angel	77
11.	Perforations	79
12.	Homeward Bound	85
13.	Floods and Drugs	93
14.	Adella	101
15.	Johnny	113
16.	Playing Piano	123
17.	Kettle Drilling	129
18.	Radishes and Cherries	135
19.	Pastor Tim Goes to Boise	143
20.	Not Destroyed	149

gunshot (n) The act of firing a gun; the discharge of a gun

gun shot (adj) The unenviable quality of having been shot with a gun

Wed, Jun 20, 2018 at 2:03 PM

Hi AmyJoy,

We may be doing a new book on the Tim Remington Story.

Tim and Cindy have agreed to record the book and we will transcribe and do the writing.

I am still working on details so this is not public info yet.

  Thu, Jun 21, 2018 at 12:19 AM

Okay, cool. I... I honestly don't know the Tim Remington story.

AJ

  Thu, Jun 21, 2018 at 11:31 AM

Pastor Tim is like the only person in the world to be shot 6 times with 45 caliber hollow points at close range and live to tell about it! And much much more....

This is not public yet so we will see how it develops before we can say much about it.

Can't wait!

David

  Thu, Jun 21, 2018 at 8:56 PM

Oh, yeah! He was joking about it at Chuck's funeral. Okay!

AJ

1

INTRODUCTION

Tim Remington came to my attention at a memorial service for the engineer-turned-Bible teacher Chuck Missler. I had done writing for the ministry of Chuck and Nancy Missler since 1999, and Chuck's death in 2018 ended an era. On June 2nd, crowds of people filled the seats at Candlelight Christian Fellowship in Coeur d'Alene, Idaho, where the old theater next to the skating rink had been converted into a church. A variety of friends stood to share memories of Chuck, then a bearded fellow with silvering hair hunched up to the podium. Pastor Tim Remington. Apparently, I'd fallen into a hole at some point, because I'd never heard of him.

"We're not of this world, are we?" Tim looked out over the audience. Then he joked, "Gotta be careful who you tell that to. Could get you shot." Laughter rippled through the room. He talked about Chuck and what he'd taught all of us, and emotion soon overwhelmed Tim. "Those were his books. That was his life," his voice cracked. "Ever since I got shot, I cry a lot. Anybody here after you get shot, cry a lot?" Again, laughter washed over the auditorium.

I got the point. This guy had been good friends with Chuck.

I'm kidding. I got the point that he'd been shot! Somebody had shot this man, and he stood on stage joking about the whole thing! Chuck Missler worked as an engineer in his early life, and gunshot victim Tim Remington reminisced about Chuck's ability to teach the mathematics of the universe as expressed in the Bible.

"It will blow you away. God uses His own physics, and Chuck Missler was the one that got me so intrigued in that stuff that I became one of you. A weirdo. People look at you like you're a weirdo... Or a reptilian." The audience laughed along with him.

I hadn't heard the story so I didn't get the joke. The man who'd shot Tim thought he was killing an alien from Mars.

A few weeks later, Dave Hanson at Chuck's ministry emailed to let me know they'd be working on Tim's story, and he wanted me on board. A year passed before the project got going, and I decided it was simplest for me to meet with Tim and his wife Cindy firsthand. I wanted to interview Jim Crabtree and John Padula and the other people involved at Tim's church. I needed freedom to ask personal, invasive questions and nitpick for details. Eventually, the ministry took its hands off the project altogether, and it was left up to the Remingtons and me.

I drove out to the Remington home above Wolf Lodge Bay, where Cindy made me coffee and told me how she and Tim had met in the first place. A week later, I munched on a chef's salad and Tim enjoyed his chocolate milkshake while I asked my questions.

I tell you this, because I didn't simply interview Tim Remington. I debated with him. I challenged Tim and poked and prodded, and he answered my challenges with honesty and grace. I met with an array of men and women who had worked through the church's drug rehabilitation programs, and I fell in love with Tim and Cindy's church family. They welcomed me into their world, and I'm deeply grateful. They're gracious and fun people, and I've reached out to them when I've needed help myself.

Amy Joy Hess
September, 2023

1
ON FIRE

Blood gushed from under him and oozed across the pavement. Rich and red, it pooled around his head and shoulders and out the sides of his ribs. He tried to move, longed to move, but the blood pinned him down and paralyzed him. Legs and shoes filled his vision, brown leather shoes and sneakers and black loafers, jeans and khakis. So much blood. It clung to him and stuck him to the ground. Something bad had happened, something horrible.

His eyes opened.

Tim Remington stared into the darkness of his bedroom. Heartbeats whooshed through his ears as he lay flat, breathing, sensing the pillow under his head and the life in his body. Three times. Three times the scene had blown through his dreams and erupted him from sleep, and concern settled with the acid in his stomach. When those images had invaded other nights, Tim awoke relieved to find the dream wasn't real. Now, he focused through darkness on the crimson puddle around his head.

"I dreamed it again," he told Cindy in the bathroom later that morning. "That dream where I'm lying in my own blood. I dreamed it again."

Cindy stood at one sink and brushed out her long strawberry hair. She paused to take in his serious face. "That dream?"

"Three times, dear." Tim raised his eyebrows at her. "This is the third time, and I think… I think I'm going to get hurt. I think God's trying to prepare me for something."

Tim didn't often dream vivid dreams, dreams he remembered. The last time he'd had a lucid dream like that, he'd seen his friend Danny serving as a missionary in Africa, married to a young lady who'd been attending their church. The dream came true. Danny married that very woman, and they eventually traveled across the world to do work in Africa. Tim had decided not to dismiss his dreams.

Tim didn't preach on March 6, 2016, the day that changed his life. He gave no loud, impressive sermon from the pulpit. He pulled into the parking lot ready to enjoy a slice or two from the pie sale that afternoon, that's all. The only thing off that morning, the only notable surprise, was a Honda Accord lodged in his parking spot. Tim usually reached the church an hour before the first service, and he always parked in the same place under the pole on the west side of the building. That was his parking spot, and all the regulars knew it. A new person had arrived extra early, though, and Tim found a silver Honda where he wanted to park. No huge deal. He drove a few yards around the building's north corner and parked there.

The congregants had been baking! Ho boy! Tim stopped between services to gaze over the table of pies - apple pies and peach pies and chocolate cream pies - set out to tempt every person who walked through the foyer. He lingered over the feast, unaware that an ill-wisher named Kyle Odom stood behind him, slim in stretchy pants, palm against the grip of his .45 caliber handgun. The security camera recorded as Tim's son Jeremiah led his own children between Tim and Kyle, unaware of the danger.

"I have no complaints, because I see the mercy of God all over that day," Tim later said. "I'm thankful Kyle didn't start shooting inside where other people could have been hurt."

Tim counseled a family in his office after the second service, and few people remained in the church at 1:45 when Tim readied himself to head out. Faithful church member Mary Jane cleaned up after the pie fest with Jim Crabtree, and surly Jack Roberts walked a final tour around the building, turning off all the lights. One by one, they walked down the foyer steps and out the front door.

M.J. was fixed on getting home to her husband. She marched past the silver Honda, unaware of the man inside. Jim Crabtree also passed the Honda without a thought.

As Jack flicked off the last lights, Tim pulled out his phone to call Cindy. The Remington family generally gathered for lunch on Sundays, and Tim rang his wife to ask where to meet. Cindy didn't answer, so Tim tried his son Jadon, who had settled with his girlfriend at the Ugly Fish Asian Bistro a few miles away. "Hi Jadon!" Tim spoke into the phone while he and Jack paused to lock the glass front doors.

March 6th, 2016. Nancy Reagan had passed away early that morning. On March 6th, 2003, 102 people aboard Air Algérie Flight 6289 perished when the 737-200 crashed shortly after takeoff. March 6th. Davy Crockett and Jim Bowie had died 180 years earlier in 1836 when the Alamo fell to Santa Anna. Tim wasn't thinking about Nancy Reagan or Davy Crockett or Algerian flight passengers as he strode past the silver car still parked in his spot. He didn't think about the other people who had died that day. Tim didn't know the driver of that Honda had been hanging out, waiting for him to appear alone and exposed, that he planned to blast Tim into the afterlife with Nancy Reagan, unfortunate Algerian travelers, and brave Texans.

At 1:54 pm on March 6th, 2016, Tim reached his car and stretched out his hand to open the door, and his world exploded in three savage seconds.

BamBamBamBamBamBamBamBamBamBamBamBam!

Across the parking lot, Jack thought kids had set off firecrackers. Jim Crabtree heard the first "pop!" and instinctively ducked behind the open door of his car. Shocked, Jack and Jim focused on a stranger in the middle of the parking lot, one leg back and solid, arms stretched before him in a shooter's stance. Kyle Odom hammered out a magazine of bullets in those three seconds, and the two men watched their pastor slam against his car and crumple to the pavement.

The first shot hit Tim mid back and smashed him into the car so hard it bruised his chest. The second bullet pierced his belt. The third, fourth, fifth, and sixth ripped through the right side of his body, one blowing through his right arm and lodging in his skull. Each bullet tore through Tim with more than 400 foot-pounds of energy, worse than blows from a 16 pound sledge hammer. Tim felt like his head had been knocked right across the parking lot.

Agony. Indescribable pain. An inferno burned through Tim, and he no longer felt individual body parts like hands and feet. His whole body blazed, as though someone had splashed gas over him and set him on fire. One bullet had nicked the lining of his right lung, and Tim gasped like a fish in a pool of fire on the ground. He moaned on the pavement and struggled to breathe as gushing blood formed a red halo around his form.

A clutter of thoughts flicked through Tim's mind. This was it, he was dying. Somebody had shot him! Who would do that? Who would shoot him? He needed his family to be there. Where was his family?

The lower half of Jim Crabtree appeared beside Tim, and his words to the 911 operator drifted down. "Jim," Tim murmured. "Please put out the fire. Put out the fire."

"Stay with me, Pastor," Jim urged. "Stay awake. Don't go to sleep. You've gotta stay awake."

Tim's phone lay on the ground still connected to Jadon. The gunfire, Jim's call to 911, his father's gurgling, all communicated horror across space to cell phone towers and down to the young man at the Ugly Fish Bistro.

Moment after moment, Tim waited for help to arrive. The fire refused to stop. On and on the agony seethed, an unrelenting cauldron of boiling rage, a merciless torment. Tim struggled to suck air while he waited, waited, for his family to appear, to kneel by him so he could talk to them one last time. He thought of his wife and his three sons and daughter. He longed to tell them he loved them before he drifted into eternity. He waited one awful minute after another. Somebody would tell his family, and they would come. Somebody had to tell them.

Neighbors and church members gathered, and Tim saw only feet and legs, brown shoes and black shoes, jeans and khakis. Not his wife. Not his kids.

The police arrived within minutes and immediately moved people back. Paramedics cut the suit from Tim's body to examine his damage, and Tim waited, desperate for Cindy to kneel beside him. He couldn't die without saying goodbye! Wait. The dream. The dream! He'd seen this ahead of time. In the dream, he'd lived.

Those night visions couldn't have prepared him for the inferno. "Make the pain stop," Tim begged, but nobody heard him. "Please stop the pain."

Tim felt everything as the paramedics did their examination. His body didn't go into the merciful land of shock. He didn't pass out. The paramedics turned him over to examine his exit wounds, and Tim listened as astonishment erupted from their mouths.

"There's a blossomed bullet in his jacket pocket," one of them wondered above him.

"What?"

"Look at this. Look. It's a blossomed bullet. I found it in his pocket."

"Here's the hole. It... it hit the suit and the vest, but stopped at his shirt."

"What?"

"It didn't go through his shirt."

"Do you see any exit wounds? I don't see any. There are no exit wounds."

"The bullets are still in him."

A bullet had made a hole in Tim's jacket, right on target for his heart. Smashed, it fell into his pocket without harming him.

"That bullet was flat," Tim later said. "Which meant it hit

something much harder than my fat. I'm not the Man of Steel."

Kyle Odom had operated under the belief that Pastor Tim Remington was an alien entity from Mars, and Kyle's mission to save Earth included killing Tim and Tim's outreach pastor John Padula. Odom had arrived that morning with a semi-automatic pistol loaded with .45 caliber hollow point cartridges. Hollow point bullets are meant to make big holes in their victims. They expand and leave cavities the size of billiard balls as they exit, bursting out guts and flesh in their departure from the body. Death follows quickly. Tim's body ferociously held onto its bullets, and not one exited after hitting his torso. Except for the bullet that shot through Tim's right arm and slammed into his head, they all stopped inside him, and his guts and flesh remained inside with them.

First responder Eric Paul kneeled over Tim with a giant needle. "Okay, listen. I have to drive this into your chest," he warned.

Tim pushed past the misery to joke, "Don't... don't you know I've been shot?"

Paul plunged the needle into Tim's pleural cavity, and - psshhhhhh - air audibly hissed as it escaped. He inserted a temporary chest tube, and Tim sucked in air, taking a full breath as his lung expanded.

During all this, Tim heard a familiar voice, one of the voices he'd been hanging on for.

"Hey! That's my dad!" As soon as Jadon heard Jim's 911 call through his father's cell phone, the young man jumped into his car and drove back to the church. He now called out from the edge of the crowd and fought to get closer, but the police held him back. They physically blocked him, and the paramedics didn't speak up to let the young man through. "You're gonna be okay, Dad!" Jadon shouted. More than anything, Tim wanted Jadon close. That was the worst thing, the worst part of it all. Tim felt the immense loss of missing out on those precious moments with his son.

The first responders weren't ready to let Tim die, though. They intravenously infused him with fluid to replace some of his lost blood. So much blood. Officer Jon Cantrell watched blood gush over the ground, as though Tim were a giant pitcher someone had dumped over. Cantrell stuck one finger into the hole in the middle of Tim's back and reached down to plug the hole at his belt line. With his right hand, Cantrell plugged three more holes in Tim's back, doing his utmost to keep the blood inside Tim's body. Wherever he could reach, he stuck a finger, and he blocked up five of Tim's wounds as he knelt on the pavement in the church parking lot. He kept his fingers in Tim's back as the paramedics moved him into their ambulance and drove him to the hospital.

Gun Shot Witness

Figure 1:1 - Credit: Mary Malone and Mike Patrick, "Pastor Gunned Down," *Coeur d'Alene Press*, March 7, 2016.   https://cdapress.com/news/2016/mar/07/pastor-gunned-down-5/

On Fire

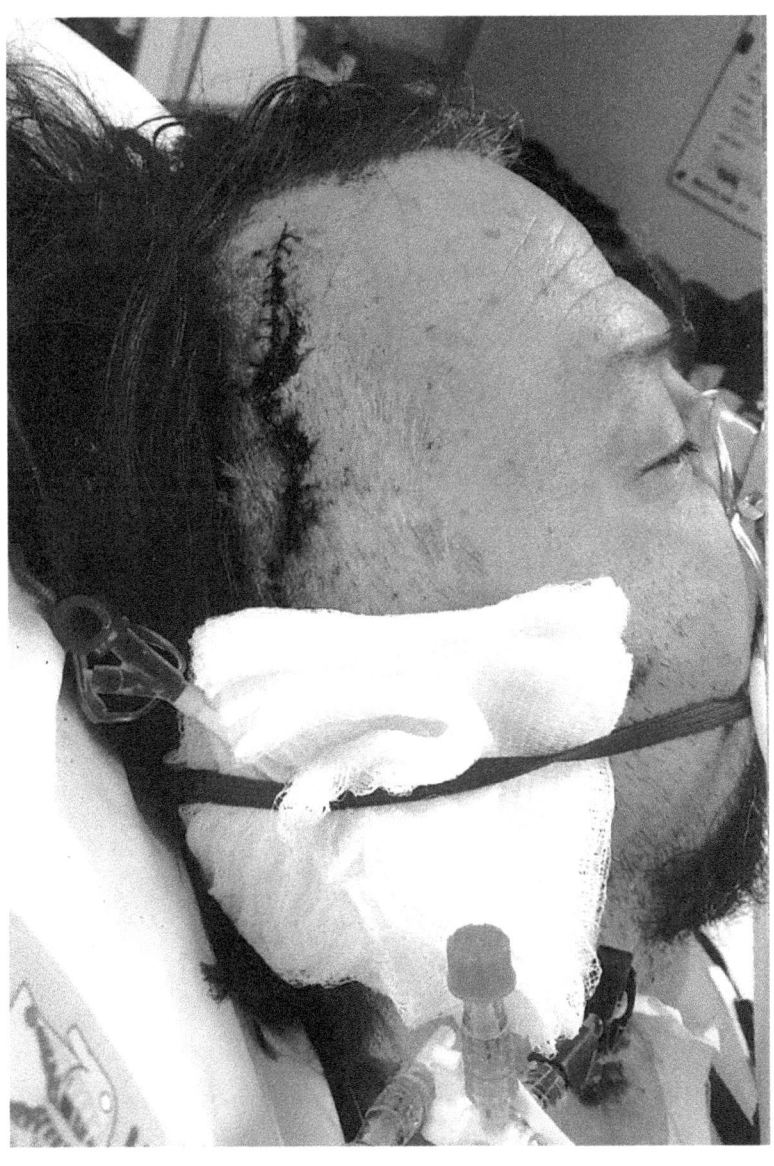

Figure 1.2 - Tim's head sutures after surgery. Photo by Julie Geist.

2
TIM AND CINDY

Tim Remington was born to a loving family in Riverside, California. His parents made their exodus to North Idaho when he was a little boy, and by 1969 they moved to a house in the hills above Wolf Lodge Bay near Coeur d'Alene. Early in Tim's childhood, his parents gave their lives to Jesus Christ, and every Sunday they took Tim to church with his brother and two sisters.

Tim grew and his world widened, and he discovered that people in his church hid the same sins as people who didn't fuss with religion. It bothered Tim that people in church looked exactly like the people he saw in the world around him. There didn't seem to be a bit of difference; they had all the same vices, the same attitudes, the same marriage problems. When Tim opened the New Testament, he saw wonderful things done in the name of Christ; people were healed and completely changed. The early church had life! Tim didn't see that life in modern churches, and it made no sense to be part of a group like that. They had no passion for the hurting people of the world. Instead, the Christians he knew all seemed afraid to reach outside their walls. They contented themselves with safety and comfort, and Tim didn't want to be that way.

Tim drank a lot during high school, chasing girls like most teenage boys. After graduation, he moved back to southern California to stay with his Uncle Lonnie, and Lonnie did little for Tim's spiritual life. Tim felt disgusted with himself, but he saw few options. Either God was real or He wasn't. Either God would change Tim's life, or He wouldn't.

Tim visited his family in Idaho in October of 1980, then he and his dog Bones took off in Tim's 1969 Dodge van to return to southern California. As he cruised down the Oregon coast, Tim decided he didn't like any of it. Christians were just as selfish as everybody else. It wasn't about God, it was about them. Everything they did, they did to make themselves look better, to make the church look better. They were working to grow money, to grow *things*. Tim didn't want anything to do with that, but he didn't like himself any better than he liked those other people.

Tim pulled over at Devil's Churn on the Oregon coast and kicked stones down a trail to the craggy ocean outlook. Sunshine shone over the expanse of blue water, the Pacific Ocean vast and open to the horizon before him. Despite the sun's cheer, a briny autumn breeze gusted Tim's ears cold as he strolled the volcanic rocks. Tim grieved that modern Christianity didn't match up with the Book of Acts. Why did Christianity today seem so stagnant, so lame, when the early disciples had been radically transformed? Tim had never seen a church filled with passion and love. He'd merely seen nice fellowships where people gathered and drank coffee.

Waves broiled in the cauldron below. As the ocean crashed, full of energy, full of life, Tim's heart loomed open and vacant – as empty as the distance between him and those salt-drenched rocks. Tim had been wired as an honorable person, but his life seemed so pointless. There was no value in any of it, and if things didn't change, he might as well fall into the swirling waters of Devil's Churn.

Tim didn't jump. He hiked back and settled into the driver's seat of his van. Bones stuck his dark head up under Tim's arm, and he rubbed behind those warm, floppy ears. Tim grabbed the steering wheel with both hands and stared through the window, not seeing the shrubs or the sky or the ocean before him.

"Lord," Tim begged with all the honesty of his heart. "If...if You're real, which I know You are, I want You to come into my life for real. For real. Do something absolutely real, Lord. If You do it, then I will be a Jesus Freak for the rest of my life. And if You don't, I'm done. I'm just done."

Tim's head lowered until it rested on the steering wheel. Those few words fell from his lips, and by the time his forehead touched the black plastic, something had changed. Something big. Life welled up inside him. During his youth, he'd gone up to the altar over and over, but this was the first time he'd fully surrendered to God, and he knew that God had done something inside him that would make all the difference.

Tim revved up his van, his blue van with the moon and stars on the side. He reached across to the passenger seat and rumpled Bones' warm ears again. That faithful dog never curled up on the carpet in the back of the van; he always rode shotgun. Tim pulled onto the road and left Devil's Churn behind, and the big "Vantastic!" across the back of his van offered his last word on the matter.

When he reached Redding, Tim stopped in at a Denny's to call his mother. "Mom! I got saved!" Six hundred miles later, back home in Redlands, Tim told his Uncle Lonnie. "We've been bad for each other. We really need to find a church."

Lonnie agreed, and in December of 1980, Tim and his uncle walked through the doors of a pretty church with a bell in the steeple, right in the middle of San Bernardino. The Loma Linda Assembly of God made a strange sight, a small country church smack in the middle of gangland, and Tim Remington with his long, hippy kid hair made a strange sight as he strolled between the pews.

The young people of Loma Linda Assembly of God stood on risers at the front of the church, colorful in their choir robes as they prepared to sing their songs. From the choir, a young woman named Marla whispered to the strawberry blonde beside her.

"Do you see that?"

Cindy watched the shaggy young man settle into his seat. "Yeah."

"What do you think?"

Cindy shrugged. "Oh. I don't know." Cindy didn't care. She had a boyfriend up north that she planned to marry one day, but after the service, she took a moment to greet the newcomer. It was the welcoming thing to do.

Cindy and Tim became easy friends, but Cindy didn't know that Tim had noticed her too, that very first day he walked into the church. He'd said to his Uncle Lonnie, "You see that girl up there? That's the girl I'm going to marry."

Lonnie laughed. "No way. I bet she won't even go out with you."

Tim had known a lot of girls, shallow girls offering shallow relationships - and he'd gladly kept it that way. When he saw Cindy, he knew somewhere deep in his knower that she was different; she was the one he'd live with for the rest of his life. And out of all the girls, she was the one who came down to shake his hand.

Tim and his uncle settled in at the Loma Linda Assembly, and Tim started showing up every time the church doors opened. He had meant it when he'd given God his life. One Wednesday evening, the pastor begged unsaved people to come up for prayer. Aged Granny Odom scooted into the pew next to Tim and said, "Son, would you please go up to the altar with me?"

"Of course I will." Tim felt the honor of being asked such a thing, to accompany this elderly lady up to the front. He moved along at her slow pace and knelt down beside her to pray. As he did, others gathered around them and laid their hands on him, and he realized, "Oh. I see what this is." Tim chuckled to himself; he looked like he needed saving.

Tim attended all the services. One night he ventured to talk to the pastor. "I'm a piano player," he explained. "Would it be okay if I play the piano softly in the background while people worship during the altar call?"

The pastor looked uncomfortable. He shook his head slowly. "I don't know if that's a good idea."

"Please. I promise I'll be respectful."

The man relented. "Okay. But, if I put my hand up, that means it's time to stop."

Tim slid quietly onto the piano bench, and he didn't break out with "Good Golly Miss Molly" or "Great Balls of Fire." He played tenderly. "And of course the pastor didn't stop him, because it was lovely," Cindy remembered.

One particular night, Tim played a song that Cindy usually sang. Because Cindy led the song service, she stood behind him as he played, and they sang it together. The harmony blended in a sweet way that moved Cindy, and that moment stuck in her mind; the two of them connected and created a nice blend. They produced worship together.

That didn't mean romance to Cindy, though. No no no. Cindy had that boyfriend up north, remember. Craig. Craig had gone away to school, and he offered her an easy way to avoid troublesome young men. "No, I can't go out with you. I've got a boyfriend away at school right now."

About this time, Craig called Cindy from across the miles. "I've realized that you're the girl I want to spend my life with. As soon as you convert, we can get married." Craig belonged to a different denomination, and Cindy had known they'd have to work out their doctrinal differences at some point, but it hadn't struck her as a big deal until this phone call. Cindy always assumed she'd end up marrying Craig, but that call gave her a moment of clarity. She didn't want to convert and join his church, and she realized that meant she couldn't marry Craig after all.

Meanwhile, Tim wouldn't stop asking her out! He even got his mother in on it.

In January, Tim's mom visited from Idaho to spend time with the improved version of her wild son. She'd rejoiced over the call from Redding, she really had, but she also took the opportunity of Tim's 20th birthday to see his change for herself.

"What do you want for your birthday?" she naturally asked.

Tim lowered his voice and pointed toward a young lady across the room. "You know what I want, Mom? What I really want? See that redhead over there? I want you to invite her out to coffee. I keep trying to take her out, but she won't go with me. If you ask her, she'll go."

"How do you tell somebody's mother 'No' on his birthday?" Cindy said. "So I went out to coffee with them."

Tim started calling Cindy every day after that, even though she technically had a "boyfriend up north." Tim had to get up at 4:00 am to fry up breakfasts as a short order cook before heading out to hang drywall all day. Still, Tim called Cindy every evening, and they'd talk until 11:00 pm as he fell asleep on the phone. Cindy didn't want to hang up on him, so she waited until he jerked awake to resume their conversations.

Within a few weeks, Tim gave Cindy a turquoise ring. She said, "I can't accept a ring from you."

"It's only a friendship ring."

Ah. Of course it is.

Cindy smiled as she described God's timing in the whole thing. As far as older, wiser Cindy was concerned, Craig up north kept away the other lads until Tim came along. Craig acted as a bookmark in Cindy's love life, holding open that page until Tim offered a life-changing prayer at Devil's Churn in Oregon and found his way into a little country church in San Bernardino.

Things turned down a more serious road in February. The youth group had been planning a "progressive dinner" for the Friday night before Valentine's Day, "a dine and dash." Zoom zoom, the youths would hop from house to house, and church members would feed the young folks one course at each stop. It gave the students a chance to eat, to have fun, and to meet a variety of adults in the church in a more personal way.

On the Wednesday before the progressive dinner, Tim attended a Bible study at Cindy's house. After the study, he headed out the door and toward his van. While Cindy stood in the doorway and watched Tim leave, he paused about 15 feet away.

"Oh. And on Friday night I'm going to ask you to marry me. Pray about it and think about it this week, and then you can have an answer for me."

They were a couple of kids who'd known each other two months. This outlandish statement startled Cindy, but she silently watched Tim climb into his van. She could have said, "Are you out of your mind!" Instead, she did what Tim asked her to do; she prayed about it and asked God to lead her. The next two days passed, and Cindy didn't know what she was going to say when Tim asked her the question. No clue.

On Friday, it seemed like Tim had forgotten all about his offhand announcement regarding the rest of their lives. Tim enjoyed people, and he busied himself talking and joking with folks as the youth group drove from house to house. He didn't seem the least bit quiet or shy or contemplative, like a normal young man preparing to ask a girl to marry him.

After the event ended and the young people dispersed, Tim and Cindy found themselves back at her house. Cindy popped into her parents' bedroom to let them know Tim was in the living room. While she was gone, Tim pushed two square coffee tables away from the couch. Cindy returned and sat next to him, and he slid onto his knees before her.

Tim took Cindy's hand and said, "Okay. I want you to think about everything you know about love."

Oh my goodness! This was it! He was proposing!

Quiet and earnest, Tim said, "Think about what your parents have taught you. Think about what the Lord has shown you. Think about what the Bible says. Think about love." He looked up at Cindy, with his shaggy brown hair and his bright brown eyes. "Do you love me?"

Until that moment, Cindy hadn't known what she was going to say. He asked her that question, and she said, "Yes."

"Will you marry me?"

She nodded, "Yes."

Tim hadn't even waited for Valentine's Day. They'd met three weeks before Christmas, and a single month had passed since Tim's mother visited for his birthday. They married four months later on June 13th, 1981, six months after Tim and Uncle Lonnie walked into that little white church.

Of course, Cindy's family members worried. Parents rarely encourage two young people, hardly adults, to jump into a lifelong commitment like that. "Hi, I met you a few minutes ago. Do you like me? Do I like you? Let's spend the rest of our lives together!"

On her wedding day, Cindy waited in the church foyer and prepared to walk down the aisle. As she stood in her wedding gown, her brother-in-law Bob approached and said, "Can I talk to you?" They walked to the side, and he said, "It's not too late, you know. Are you sure you want to do this? You can still call it off." The family liked Tim, "Vantastic" van and all. Still, Bob asked her that hard but important question.

Looking back, Cindy said, "Bob had a lot of chutzpah to come up and offer me an out." But, she believed ever after she made the right decision. She loved Tim.

Cindy walked down the aisle minutes later, and at the end stood Tim and his 6'4" father. Tears dripped down the cheeks of both men as she approached the altar. All went well until it was time to light the unity candle. As Tim's sisters sang, Cindy and Tim held their two single candles out and ... they realized somebody had forgotten to place the unity candle up there for them.

"The candle isn't there," Tim whispered.

"I know. What do we do?" Cindy whispered back.

"Let's just hold the candles together." So, that's what they did. They touched their candles, one to another, and the flames joined and made one large, bright light.

And that – that became the story of their lives.

Figure 2:1 - Tim and Cindy in 1984, courtesy of Cindy Remington.

3
THE FAMILY

Jadon didn't think his dad would make it. Tim and Cindy had four children: Jeremiah, Josiah, Jadon, and Gracie. Of the family members, only Jadon experienced the shooting personally, and his dreams tormented him for months after. On the phone, he'd heard what sounded like somebody banging on a metal door - bam bam bam - and then the gurgles and Jim Crabtree's call to 911. He'd immediately jumped into his car and raced to the church, where he saw his dad collapsed in a puddle of blood. All that blood. Jadon watched on as the paramedics did their work and hurriedly got on his phone to notify his mother. She didn't answer, so he called his oldest brother.

While Kyle Odom emptied his gun on her husband, Cindy Remington pushed a cart through the Coeur d'Alene WinCo Foods with three of the girls she was mentoring. She hadn't turned her phone up after the church service, so she didn't hear Tim's call to ask where they were eating lunch. She didn't hear Jadon's call or Jeremiah's call or the call from M.J. As Cindy left the grocery store, she checked her phone and saw that half a dozen people had tried to contact her. First, Cindy called Tim, but he didn't answer. Next, she called Jadon.

"Hello Jadon," she said.

Jadon answered in the car on his way to the hospital. "Mom, Dad's been shot."

Cindy thought he was giving her a hard time because she hadn't answered earlier. Her kids would do that if she didn't pick up; they'd say, "Mom. I could have been in a ditch. You've got to start answering your phone." Cindy quickly apologized.

"I know, I know, Jadon. I'm sorry. I didn't turn on my phone after service."

"Mom." Jadon repeated, "Dad's been shot."

"Jadon."

"Mom, listen. Listen. Dad has been shot. I'm on my way to the hospital. You need to go there right now. I don't know how he is. He was alive when they put him in the ambulance."

A surge of adrenaline. Tension pumped through Cindy, but she turned to the three girls and calmly told them, "Ladies, we're on our way to the hospital. Tim has been shot. I don't know what the facts are."

Cindy worked her way down the line of missed calls and rang M.J. next, but M.J. just handed the phone to Jim Crabtree. Jim immediately jumped into telling Cindy what he'd seen - the shooting, the paramedics, the silver Honda - but that's not what Cindy wanted to know. Finally, she interrupted him. "Jim, I don't care about any of that. I just need to know if Tim is okay. How is he?"

Jim got quiet. "I don't know. I called 911, but I'm sorry, I really don't know."

Jadon had already called Jeremiah and Gracie, but nobody could reach Josiah. Josiah had gone to visit friends in Kooskia, Idaho, nearly 200 miles away in the land of no cell reception. They had no way to contact him, until Tim's mom remembered that Josiah had called her from a landline that weekend. Grandma gave Jeremiah the number, and Josiah raced the winding roads through the mountains and arrived within hours.

The hospital workers refused to let the family see Tim, though. Cindy and the kids waited with no answers, unable to stand beside him, hold his hand, tell him they loved him. Hospital staff held them back and kept them out. "We need to get him stabilized."

Before Tim went into surgery, the doctors ordered a CT scan, and one compassionate nurse took advantage of that opportunity.

The Family

She worried this might be the last chance Tim's family had to see him alive, so she rushed in and told them to follow her.

"Okay guys. Come with me. You can see him for a moment." She moved them quickly down the hospital halls and into a little room.

Cindy walked through the door and saw her damaged husband for the first time. The medical staff readied Tim for his scan as his broken body lay limp on the gurney. Blood from Tim's head had gushed over his face and clothes, matting in his hair and beard. Cindy walked to his side and rested her hand on him, and he managed a whisper.

"The pain."

"I'm so sorry," Cindy said.

"You need to make it stop."

"I know, dear. I'm so sorry."

"Tell the kids I love them."

"I will." Cindy's hand remained on her husband, a simple touch, one comfort she could offer in those moments. "Do you understand what happened?"

Tim barely shook his head.

"You got shot."

In spite of all that suffering, Tim's personality pushed through. He raised his eyebrows and said, "Well, I figured that much." Then he whispered, "Who?"

"You mean, who shot you?"

He gave a slight nod. The agony continued on and on, every moment as awful as the one before, and Tim's head shake was barely a shake, and his nod was barely a nod.

"We don't know. We have no idea yet."

Nobody had recognized Kyle Odom. Jack had run after the Honda to get its license plate number, but as Cindy stood by her suffering husband, Kyle drove south to Boise to board a plane for Washington D.C. Two days later, he flung materials over the White House fence for President Obama - earning the strong disapprobation of the Secret Service.

27

Jim Crabtree did remember the Honda. He'd seen it before. Jim drove a taxi, and he'd pulled into the church parking lot at 2:00 am to use the church's Wifi. While he drove in, he saw a strange silver car parked there. He hadn't thought much of it at the time, but church surveillance video later revealed that Kyle Odom had scoped out the church several times before the Sunday he shot Tim.

It's interesting that Kyle used Tim's parking spot the morning of March 6th. The camera on that side of the church was out, and the surveillance system would have been blind to the shooting if Tim had parked in his regular spot. The whole event was captured only because Tim parked around the north side of the church where the cameras were working. They recorded Tim as he walked to his car. They recorded as Kyle stepped forward, took his shooter's stance, and pounded Tim with bullets. The cameras watched as Jim ran over to Tim and called 911.

The doctors finished the CT scan and pushed Tim out from behind the curtain. As they wheeled him by, he finally had the thing he'd wanted most since the shooting: his family near him. Cindy and three of their grown children lined up along the wall. As the gurney rolled by, Tim finally enjoyed a few precious moments with his kids.

"We love you. We love you, Dad," they repeated over and over again as he passed them.

"Love you guys. Love you."

Those were important, sweet moments, and nobody knew whether they were the last they'd all have together. As they wheeled Tim away for surgery, Dr. Robert G. Holman met Cindy in the hallway. "I don't know what we're going to find when we get in there. I can't make any promises, but we'll do our best."

Tim had lost nine pints of blood. Nine. Average adult humans have 10-13 pints circulating through their bodies, and after losing only 40% of blood volume, systolic blood pressure drops dangerously. There's just not enough pressure to move the remaining blood through the necessary miles of vessels. The heart pumps faster and faster, struggling to force life's fluid to vital organs, and the victim quickly succumbs to exsanguination – "bleeding out." Weakness, confusion, coma, and death quickly follow the loss of six pints or more. The fluids provided by the paramedics gave him that precious extra time, but Tim defied reason by surviving and remaining conscious.

Tim should have died on the pavement outside the church. He should have died in the ambulance with Officer Cantrell's fingers plugged into him. He should have died in surgery, but that evening he pushed on and on as one surgeon after another worked to repair the eight holes caused by six bullets. Tim survived the operations and repair work, and he kept living after they wheeled him out of surgery late that night.

"People expected to see a big old 'S' on my shirt."

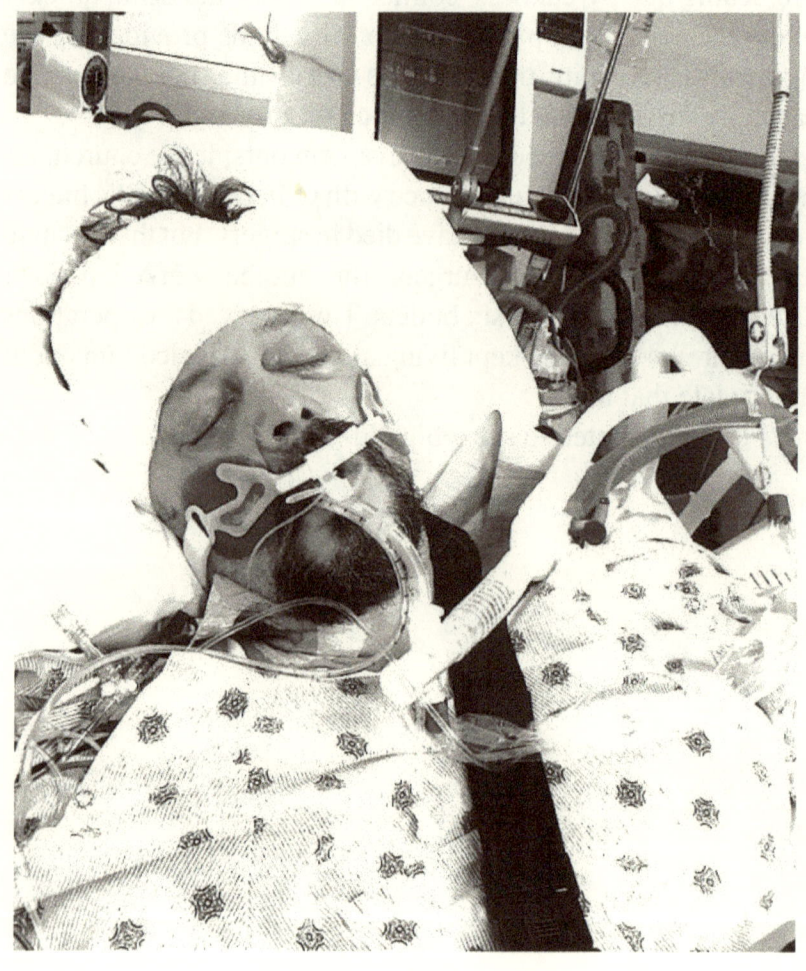

Figure 3.1 - Tim Remington surgically repaired and bandaged. Photo by Julie Geist.

Jeremiah Remington, right, listens to his brother, Josiah, talk on Thursday at Kootenai Health about the recovery of their father, Tim, a pastor who was shot at least six times on Sunday in The Altar Church parking lot in Coeur d'Alene. "He's on the healing track," Josiah said of his father's recovery.

Pastor upgraded to stable condition

Remington may remain in hospital for weeks after being shot at least six times

By BRIAN WALKER
Staff Writer

COEUR d'ALENE — Pastor Tim Remington is making strides in recovery, even joking at times,

Remington, pastor of The Altar Church in Coeur d'Alene, remained in the intensive care unit at Kootenai Health and was upgraded to stable condition on Thursday. He was in serious condition on Wednesday.

"He is on the healing track and not going backward," said Josiah Remington, a son of Tim's. "We are so grateful for the prayers

"He can talk, but is not talking much due to the pain medication and he's trying to rest," Jeremiah said. "He has no brain trauma and his mental state is 100 percent."

Kyle Odom, 30, of Coeur d'Alene, allegedly shot the pastor in the parking lot of the church. Odom flew to Washington, D.C., on Monday from Boise and was

Figure 3.2 - Credit: Brian Walker, "Pastor Upgraded to Stable Condition," *Coeur d'Alene Press,* March 11, 2016.   https://cdapress.com/news/2016/mar/11/pastor-upgraded-to-stable-condition-5/

4
GSWs

When Air Algérie Flight 6289 crashed shortly after takeoff on March 6, 2003, 102 people lost their lives. All the crew and passengers died - all but one. You see, 102 people perished, but *103* had boarded that flight. The 28-year-old Algerian soldier Youcef Djillali had been sitting in the final row without his seat belt on, and he ejected from the plane when it smashed into the ground. He awoke from a coma the next day, the lone survivor.

Youcef had reason to regard his survival as a miracle, but if one is going to survive a plane crash, it's statistically best to be sitting in the far back of the plane. Of 20 crashes in the United States between 1971 and 2007, 69% of those seated in the back were able to return to their families.[1]

What are the statistics on surviving a gunshot wound (GSW)? More specifically, what are the odds of surviving five .45 caliber hollow point bullets through the torso, where so many major organs are packed together? What are the odds of surviving a bullet to the head? Bam! Worse than getting hit with a sledgehammer?

According to the FBI, 11,138 firearm homicides occurred in the United States in 2016, of which 7,204 were committed using handguns.[2] A *Preventative Medicine* study averaged the number

---
1 David Nolan, "What is the Safest Seat on a Plane?" *Popular Mechanics* (July 18 2007).
2 FBI, "Expanded Homicide Data Table 8: Murder Victims by Weapon, 2013–2017," *2017 Crime in the United States*, https://ucr.fbi.gov/crime-in-the-u.s/2017/crime-in-the-u.s.-2017/tables/expanded-homicide-data-table-8.xls.

of gun-related homicides between 2010 and 2012 and found that 11,256 people died while 48,534 people were non-fatally injured in assaults with firearms each year.[3] This suggests that 1/5 of firearm attacks are fatal – on average.

That's not nearly good enough, though. These statistics don't tell us what caliber of gun was used or how many times the victims were shot or what parts of the body were impacted. A multitude of factors determine whether a gunshot wound kills its victim. The size of the bullet, its velocity, its cartridge and jacket and where it hits the body all make a difference. When the bullets hit arms or legs, their victims generally recover if they don't bleed to death. One study found that 83% of those with GSW liver injuries survived if they were stitched up quickly,[4] but the injuries to the liver were minor in 105 of the study's 153 cases.[5] Twelve of the 13 who perished after a liver GSW died from uncontrolled bleeding.

If a bullet damages its victim's brain or spine, the main components of the central nervous system (CNS), that person's usually a goner. In certain studies, 90% of people shot in the head died before reaching the hospital.[6][7] According to researchers:

> In the head and torso, there are organs and structures in which almost any anatomic disruption will result in death, e.g., the CNS, heart, and great vessels, whereas structures in the extremities are typically more tolerant of gunshot injuries.[8]

---

3   Katherine A Fowler, Linda Dahlberg, Tadesse Haileyesus and Joseph Annest, "Firearm injuries in the United States," *Preventative Medicine* 79 (2015):5-14, doi:10.1016/j.ypmed.2015.06.002.
.4   JD Marr, JE Krige, J Terblanche, "Analysis of 153 gunshot wounds of the liver," *The British Journal of Surgery* 87, no 8 (2000):1030-4, doi: 10.1046/j.1365-2168.2000.01487.x.
5   Ibid.
6   R. Cavaliere, L. Cavenago, D Siccardi, GL Viale, "Gunshot Wounds of the Brain in Civilians," *Acta Neurochir (Wien)* 94, no. 3-4 (1988):133e136, doi: 10.1007/BF01435866.
.7   M. Shaffrey, R. Polin, C. Phillips, et al., "Classification of Civilian Cranio-Cerebral Gunshot Wounds: a Multivariate Analysis Predictive of Mortality," *Journal of Neurotrauma* 9 (1992):S279eS285.
8   Jowan G. Penn-Barwell, Kate V. Brown and C.A. Fries, "High Velocity Gunshot Injuries to the Extremities; Management On and Off the Battlefield," *Current Reviews in Musculoskeletal Medicine* 8, no 3 (2015): 312-317, doi: 10.1007/s12178-015-9289-4.

Every shooting is a unique event that can't be replicated, which makes statistics difficult. It's no good comparing apples and oranges. The rapper 50 Cent survived in 2000 after he was shot nine times with 9 mm bullets, but he wasn't shot in the core of his body; the bullets slammed through his legs, hand, and jaw. They broke his legs in multiple places but left his major arteries intact. It's wonderful he lived through the experience, and it's legitimate to say, "Hey, it's a miracle 50 Cent is with us," but the survival rate for people shot in the legs is much higher than those shot center of mass. That makes sense.

In movies, characters constantly want to dig out the bullet when their buddy is shot. Actors hold up a trespassing gob of lead, and everyone seems content the victim will heal. That bloody chunk offers a satisfying plot picture for audiences, but it's minor in reality. Gunshot victims walk around for decades with bullets lodged inside them. The journey the bullet took before it stopped, that's what makes all the difference between serious injury and life or death. Chunks of lead can bounce around inside their victims, ripping apart organs and arteries until blood gushes. Whether they're bleeding internally or externally, that blood loss is a death sentence.

There are two primary injuries caused by bullets, both potentially lethal:

First, there are the permanent cavities, the holes created by the physical bullets. These are the wounds we all imagine as metal cuts and shears its path through the body.

Second, there's a temporary cavity caused by the shock wave from each bullet. Remember, a bullet isn't a nice sharp knife. It's a projectile that tears through flesh at high speeds. The kinetic energy of the bullet is transferred to the surrounding tissue as it passes through, which creates a cavitation bubble, a cavity that expands several centimeters wider than the physical bullet. It expands and collapses back on itself, which causes additional damage. The higher the bullet velocity, the bigger the temporary cavity, the bigger the shock wave, the more traumatic the effects on the surrounding tissue.

It also matters a lot where the bullet strikes. That metal missile can break and pulverize bone while soft muscle tissue flexibly stretches and collapses back with less damage. On the other hand, a high-powered shock wave through the kidneys can turn the surrounding cells to jelly.

Bullets with a "full metal jacket" hold soft lead inside but are encased in a hard material, usually a copper alloy. They remain fairly intact as they enter their victims, and the bullets tend to pass through and exit. A bullet that deforms or fragments or tumbles around is going to do a lot more damage than a mini-spear that shoots straight out the other side. Hollow point bullets deform and expand on entry, creating much larger permanent and temporary cavities.

On March 6, 2016, six large, brutal .45 caliber hollow point bullets smashed through the body of Tim Remington. They should have turned his body to mush. The human trunk is filled with vital organs that bullets tend to rip apart: heart, lungs, liver, spleen, kidneys, stomach. Hollow points blossom into large metal chunks that tear and mangle soft tissue, and death arrives in minutes.

It might be better to face a plane crash.

In an interesting contrast, on March 6th of 1981, a woman walked into a courtroom in Germany and shot Klaus Grabowski, the man on trial for raping and strangling her seven-year-old little girl. Marianne Bachmeier pulled out a .22-caliber Beretta pistol and fired eight shots at her daughter's confessed killer as he walked away. Six of those bullets pierced Grabowski, who collapsed right there in the courtroom. Though small, .22 bullets can bounce around inside their victims, and Grabowski died almost immediately. Six bullets hit Grabowski in the back at close range and killed him that 6th of March. Thirty-five years later to the day, six bullets hit Tim Remington in the back and head at close range. The bullets that hit Tim were meaner and much larger, creating significantly bigger permanent and temporary cavities, yet Grabowski died and Tim lived.

Since the shooting, Tim has searched unsuccessfully for another recorded case in which somebody survived multiple body shots with .45 hollow points. Those folks might exist, but he was unable to track them down.

Tim's survival was remarkable. The five bullets that hit his torso didn't tear apart his vital organs. The shot to his head didn't touch his brain. He reached the hospital knocked down, torn and devastated - but not destroyed.

Figure 4.1 - A .22 LR cartridge next to a .45 ACP hollow point cartridge for comparison.

5
Miracles on the Edge

Tim Remington's shooting made the evening news on March 6th. During the 11:00 broadcast, KXLY 4 News showed footage of congregants gathered in the parking lot of the church, holding hands in a circle to seek God on behalf of their cherished pastor.

"Many here have come together to pray for a friend left fighting for his life," KXLY reported. "Just a few hours earlier, near tragedy, Pastor Tim Remington was shot several times as he was leaving The Altar Church."

Outreach Pastor John Padula told KXLY, "There's a lot of people hurting really bad right now over this, but a lot of people who are believing that God has a plan."

KXLY continued, "Friends of Remington say he's the type of guy who would reach out to help anyone facing a dark time in their life. They say he's helped some 1700 people over the years."

"Most of them are addicts," John Padula explained. "Addicted to something, just totally lost. And him and his wife and family have given up their lives to minister to all of us hope and help us find hope in Jesus…We trust God, we trust Jesus, that He's going to work something miraculous through this."

KXLY's John Henricks finished up the story: "Church members told me tonight Remington is out of surgery, he has no brain or spinal damage, and that he's expected to make a full recovery."

Those were strong words. For the first week, doctors weren't completely certain that Tim would pull through. Not for lack of prayer. A prayer vigil formed spontaneously in the Kootenai Medical Center in Coeur d'Alene, and visitors backed up to the hospital cafeteria that afternoon as hundreds of people showed up to check on their pastor. Meanwhile, John Padula worked hard to protect Tim from the news media.

And not for lack of love. The local community came out in great compassion and creativity to provide help for Tim Remington. Coeur d'Alene screen printing shop Lo-Go immediately printed "Praying for Pastor Tim" shirts, which they sold as a fundraiser toward Tim's medical expenses. Best Buzz coffee chose a Saturday to give 50% of its sales to Tim. May 1st, more than 800 people attended a fundraiser for Tim at the Coeur d'Alene Resort. The *Coeur d'Alene Press* took out a full page on May 11, 2016 to thank the hundreds of people and businesses who had donated their time, services and products for Tim's benefit. Shaggy young Tim Remington had apparently accomplished what was always in his heart- to make a real impact on the world in God's love, and the community did its best to look after him when it mattered.

And nobody missed the reality that God had protected this goofy, bearded pastor. Tim later noted, "You know, we didn't have a huge prayer meeting before the shooting. We didn't know anything was going to happen that particular day. We didn't have to jump through hoops. God in His sovereignty saved my life. We know that the hand of God was in it, and He did it all."

"It's a miracle that you're alive."

"It's a miracle that this bullet didn't hit your spine or take out your lung."

"It's a miracle that bullet didn't go through your colon."

"It's a miracle this bullet didn't hit your heart."

"It's a miracle that the bullet in your skull didn't hit your brain."

Tim lived despite the holes and blood loss, despite the nerve damage and the bullet to his head. The EMTs, the doctors, the nurses all agreed that Tim's survival truly fit into the category of the miraculous.

Dr. Robert Holman acted as head physician in Tim's operating room. On his last day before retirement, his last hoorah, Dr. Holman worked with one surgeon after another to patch Tim up, and he noted with awe that Tim had more than 100 pieces of shrapnel in his body, yet all his organs remained intact.

"If you want evidence of a miracle, that's it," Dr. Holman told Cindy.

During Tim's seven hours in surgery, a liaison nurse came out at intervals to tell Cindy and the family what had been going on. Each step in the surgery process caused another round of astonishment as the doctors involved took turns at Tim's repair. They all offered new perspectives on the wonders involved in Tim's survival and recovery based on their own areas of expertise.

The first bullet missed Tim's spine by millimeters and nicked the lining of his lung. The surgeons left it in there; it would be more damaging to take it out than to leave it.

The second bullet pierced his belt and made a hole through the thinnest part of his pelvic bone. It curved into his belly, where it missed his stomach and intestines before it came to a stop. That one remained in him too.

Two of the three bullets in his upper back worked their way up to the surface months later, and surgeons were able to remove those from his brachial plexus. The third stayed behind, a stubbornly content squatter. Three bullets in total remained a relatively permanent part of Tim's person, along with 100-odd pieces of shrapnel. Tim would never again be able to slide into an MRI machine. He had to walk through a special scanner every time he visited the airport.

The liaison nurse told Cindy that when orthopedic surgeon Dr. Jonathan Linthicum opened Tim's arm, all those around the operating table hung their heads and took a step back, because that bullet had totally obliterated Tim's right humerus. In a battlefield setting, medics might have sawed off the pulverized arm, but Dr. Linthicum didn't give up. He decided to treat the tiny fragments of bone as pieces to a puzzle. Shard by shard, those pieces came together.

Dr. Linthicum explained to Cindy that he normally sees just a few pieces of bone, and his job required that he put those together and set them. In Tim's case, the bone had been blown to dust and tiny fragments, as though somebody had taken a coffee mug and wrapped it in duct tape and then hammered it and hammered it. There was no way. However, God is in the empowerment business, and Dr. Linthicum believed the Lord gave him the ability to put those pieces of bone back together. He had to hold it all together with pins, but the surgery saved Tim's right arm.

"We all watched in awe as it came together," said the nurse.

Cindy overheard a conversation between two doctors after Dr. Holman removed the bullet from Tim's skull. The surgeon beckoned to the Remington's family physician in the Intensive Care Unit the next day. Dr. Holman and Dr. Terrance Riske huddled in the corner, like two little boys whispering together, unaware that Cindy could hear them.

Dr. Holman said to Dr. Riske, "I pulled out the bullet, and I saw the dura."

"You saw it?" Dr. Riske said, astonished.

"I saw it! I pulled out the bullet and there was the dura!"

The bullet that smashed through Tim's skull, through layers of bone, had stopped right at the soft tissue. The dura mater is the outer layer of the meninges, the thick membrane that surrounds the brain, and that's where the bullet halted – as though Tim's meninges were made of Kevlar.

"It was just funny. These two doctors over in the corner, whispering. Then they came strolling back over, all cool." Cindy smiled.

Tim survived the many surgeries, but after days in the ICU, the hospital staff still couldn't declare him free and clear. They had him on a respirator for several days, forcing air into his lungs, keeping him alive as his devastated body began the exhausting work to heal its damage.

Years later, Tim couldn't think of the respirator without horror.

"He hated it," Cindy said with emotion. "He hated the respirator. He hated it." She paused to think of another way to put it, but she finished, "He hated it." The respirator forced him to breathe in and forced him to breathe out, giving Tim a claustrophobic panic. Helpless, without strength to fight for himself, Tim suffered for days through the anxiety of having no control over his own lungs. When they finally removed the respirator days later, Tim sucked in air and released it again in vast relief.

Meanwhile, Cindy sat with Tim day after day in remarkable calm, thankful every moment that he had survived. "And then I was grateful he was alive. And then he passed out against me, and I was grateful he was alive."

Only one occasion sparked fear in Cindy: the day that Tim - off the respirator - stopped breathing.

Cindy remained with Tim constantly, always right beside him. One week after the shooting, he asked her, "Who is preaching today?"

"Pastor Kurt is preaching."

"Okay good." Tim closed his eyes. Then he opened them again and looked at his wife of nearly 35 years. "I love you."

"I love you too."

"You're doing a good job."

"Thank you, dear."

Tim closed his eyes, and a funny sound began to gurgle in his throat. Concerned, Cindy rose and looked into the hall. She quickly found a male nurse and brought him in. The nurse examined Tim and said, "He's just snoring. Do you want me to wake him up?"

"No…" Cindy felt like something had changed, something was off, but she didn't want to take Tim from much-needed sleep.

"Let me know if anything goes wrong? He's just asleep and snoring," the nurse insisted.

Cindy sat with Tim, but as she watched him, she wasn't convinced the nurse had been right. A couple of seconds went by, and Tim's chest hung still. No air entered to make it rise, and no air exited to make it fall. Five seconds passed, and he wasn't breathing. Ten seconds passed.

Cindy called again for help, and the hospital staff sauntered in. In a moment they realized Tim's danger, and a flurry of activity exploded in the room. They pressed an accordion-like apparatus on his mouth to breathe for him, and soon they intubated him again, forcing his lungs to expand and contract.

This was the one moment Cindy thought, "Lord, You've brought him through so much. You saved his life in the shooting, the loss of blood, the surgeries, the rebuilding… and now? Now?" She hadn't feared for Tim's life the whole previous week. In one moment, she felt the shock, the jolt of, "Wait? Am I losing him?"

As soon as the staff had stabilized her husband, Cindy retreated to the bathroom to hide after the stress of the moment. She sat on the toilet and, for the first time since Tim had been shot, Cindy dropped her face into her hands and bawled.

6
KYLE ODOM

> Police say Kyle Odom feared Martians when he shot an Inland native in Idaho.
>
> By NICHOLAS K. GERANIOS
> THE ASSOCIATED PRESS

The day before Kyle Odom shot him, Tim had offered the opening prayer at a Ted Cruz presidential campaign rally, and people guessed the shooter had political motivations. No, that wasn't it. Kyle wanted to stop aliens from Mars. Kyle Andrew Odom shot Pastor Tim Remington because he believed that Tim was a Martian pawn garbed up in human skin.

Many have assumed that Kyle Odom just went crazy. He was a bright young man who suffered ongoing auditory, visual, and physical hallucinations. He was nuts. That was the reasonable place to start, of course. There were clues that something else, something more sinister was going on, however. At least, Tim didn't think Kyle simply suffered from a mental breakdown.

"I've never felt angry with Kyle Odom," Tim said. "He was a brilliant kid who got into eastern meditation. He doesn't have mental problems: he has a spiritual problem."

Kyle wrote a 43-page manifesto, delivered by post to his parents and local news outlets after the shooting. That manifesto provides a small view of the torment Kyle struggled through before he resorted to murder.

Kyle was raised by a loving family in North Idaho and served in the U.S. Marines from 2006 to 2010. He went on to study biochemistry at the University of Idaho, and he started meditating every day to deal with the stresses of his heavy course load. During the Spring 2014 semester, he regularly practiced his meditation techniques to develop more "extreme states of consciousness." One day while meditating, he left his body in an out-of-body experience and encountered another being. Kyle felt blissful, unconditional love from this being, but he found he could no longer meditate after he woke up. In his manifesto, Kyle explains that he finished his final semester with ease, as though his mind had expanded and grown open to more knowledge.

Kyle graduated magna cum laude and was accepted to a graduate program in genetics at Baylor University in Waco, Texas. The research disappointed him, though; he claims that he saw flaws in all the research because of his mentally enlightened state. Nobody else seemed to care (which raises the possibility that those "flaws" may have been in Kyle's head). He felt he was wasting his time, so he left. Soon after that, Kyle writes that amphibian-humanoid beings in the form of humans began to follow him.

Kyle describes how he was tormented after leaving Baylor by an ancient race of hyper-aggressive, hyper-sexual Martians. He claims to have talked to the entities and learned about them over a long period of time. They told him they had destroyed their own planet and now inhabited Earth, where they used humans as a breeding stock. They told Kyle they owned certain humans, who were raised and controlled since birth and had no minds of their own but could be used like puppets or remote controlled robots. The aliens eventually told Kyle that Pastors Tim Remington and John Padula fit into this group.

According to Kyle, the Martians use "wild" humans as sex slaves – humans not under their direct mental control. He states that Martians followed and harassed him constantly, because they were unable to take control of his mind. He believed that Martian-controlled humans lived at every level of society, including the highest levels of government, and his manifesto lists members of the U.S. Senate and House of Representatives, both Republican and Democrat, as Martians. The malicious entities boasted to Kyle about the things they did to President Barack Obama, and his manifesto includes cloaked messages to the president. On Tuesday, March 8, 2016, two days after shooting Tim, Kyle was arrested in Washington D.C. after tossing flash drives and other materials over the fence at the White House.

Psychologist Dr. Paul Domitor reviewed Kyle's manifesto with KXLY's Allie Norton. He recognized Kyle's intelligence but told KXLY that paranoid schizophrenia is "a terrible illness. It's heartbreaking to the family. People just come apart."

Odom's manifesto does read like an intelligent person suffering from severe schizophrenia, a man experiencing the world through a film of paranoia and an inflated sense of his mental superiority. He describes strange things. He explains that he encountered human-looking Martians constantly. On airplanes. In grocery stores. They sniffed at him forcefully, which he saw as a show of dominance. Kyle states, "As you can see, I'm pretty smart. I'm also 100% sane, 0% crazy." He then goes on to describe what sounds like a descent into paranoid madness.

Kyle believed that the aliens were furious and targeted him because they couldn't control his mind, but his own testimony describes their ability to infiltrate his thoughts. They repeatedly put their ideas into his head and denied him sleep with repetitive songs: "Sister, sister. He's just a plaything. We wanna make him stay up all night." They sexually molested him, giving him no rest, filling him with terror until he couldn't function normally.

There are a few ways to look at Kyle's story - a few different possible explanations:

1) He was a smart young man who didn't recognize the onset of a mental disorder and suffered untreated for two years until he shot somebody.

2) His story is completely true, and Martians followed him and made his life miserable.

3) He was being followed by malevolent entities that were

not actually Martians, that is, evil beings that lied to Kyle about their true identities.

4) Kyle suffered a combination of both mental and spiritual problems - mental instability and harassment by actual entities.

First, it's clear from his manifesto that Kyle was not operating with full reasoning skills, starting with his view that the Martians feared his brain power. Kyle was a decent writer and researcher, and he could summarize the views of the scientific majority on cosmology and ancient history, but it was silly of him to conclude that his human mind would threaten a race he claimed had technology millions of years older than his. If they were able to telepathically communicate, pop in and out of our dimensionality, and materialize items from nowhere, it's unlikely his intelligence would have impressed them. Kyle had an inflated view of his own intellect, which made him a prime target for deception. As Proverbs 16:18 says, pride goes before destruction (and a haughty spirit before a fall).

Kyle offered other lapses in logic. For instance, he believed an older man on a plane was trying to communicate to him without words. He states:

> Once we landed, the older gentleman kept showing me his TracFone as if to say, "Get one of these." I had applied to several government agencies before this happened, so I thought this might be their way of contacting me.

The FBI and NSA and CIA application processes are long and involved. If they liked Kyle's application, they'd reach out to him for interviews and physical and mental evaluations before accepting him as a new recruit. Kyle Odom had nearly reached age 30 when all these things started taking place. He wasn't a 12-year-old with an overactive imagination. He'd gone through the military. If he were operating under full mental health, he wouldn't have made those kinds of unreasonable connections.

Kyle had a range of bizarre ideas in his aggravated mental state. He visited Tim's church The Altar because he thought the government was using the church as a recruiting center. Then, suddenly, he was convinced that extraterrestrials were involved. That's a big leap. He says:

> When the service began a man came and sat down next to me. After he sat down, I began smelling something. It was a smell I had never smelt before. The only thing I can compare it to is a reptile and vinegar. After smelling it, I became very uncomfortable. I tried to remain calm and just sat there quietly until the service was over... After that, I knew I wasn't dealing with the government anymore. I realized that whoever I was dealing with was extraterrestrial, so I became very scared.

Kyle's erratic descriptions of events without any context and his constant terror over small things hardly give readers confidence in his mental stability.

Let's say we take him at face value, though. Let's suggest for a moment that Kyle Odom was being hounded by cruel entities that enjoyed his pain, and his terror and paranoia were understandable results of that abuse.

Part of the problem of reading through Kyle's manifesto is determining which events physically took place and which events were all in his mind. When the entities sexually molested him, it was painful and he couldn't sleep because of it. Whatever the true cause, this was an ongoing source of suffering that Kyle really experienced. On the other hand, Kyle claims that two other graduate students reached out to him after he left Baylor, and when he met with them, they pointed at him with their fingers, saying, "Pew pew pew." He later "learned" they weren't humans; they were charged with the job of making Kyle into the next school shooter. Were the students he saw real people? Was he hallucinating? Either way, the entirety of his experience ironically succeeded in turning him into a shooter after all.

Kyle claims to have visited The Altar several times and to have talked to Tim in person. While they were chatting, Kyle says that Tim manifested as his alien self for a few seconds:

> ...I found myself talking to Tim Remington face to face. He was telling me that I should consider becoming a minister. We were in mid conversation when he suddenly revealed himself to me. I have no clue how he did it, but it looked as if his human face became his real face. It happened for only 1-2 seconds, but I was able to draw a sketch of what I saw. His eyes really stood out so they

Figure 6.2 - Tim Remington the alien, as portrayed by Kyle Odom in his manifesto.

captured my attention. They were huge and bulging, the eyelids were darker green, and the irises were yellow/brown with slit pupils.

Tim doesn't recall ever talking to Kyle face to face before the shooting. He did remember seeing him on that March 6th, but only because Kyle wore spandex and John Padula had said to Tim, "Hey. You should dress like that." That was Tim's only memory of Kyle.

Kyle's problems might not have been merely neurological, though. There were indications that something else was going on, something that went beyond brain chemistry. Tim believed Kyle opened up a spiritual doorway through transcendental meditation, and Kyle had been demonically oppressed ever since.

While there are things that suggest Kyle's mental health had deteriorated, there are several things that also support Tim's view. Kyle's "aliens" match the known characteristics of unclean spirits. Kyle claimed to be beyond the alien mind control, and yet they tortured him constantly by putting their ideas into his head. Like demons, Kyle's "Martians" are:

-interdimensional beings;
-able to materialize items out of nowhere;
-arrogant, cruel, and abusive;
-loveless;
-hyper-sexual and hyper-aggressive;
-obsessed with power and domination;
-paranoid and fearful.

Some indicators of Kyle's spiritual oppression were his hostile views on God and the Bible. He wrote that there was no God, that the aliens invented the idea of God to control primitive humans. He wrote that, "Jesus was a megalomaniacal fraud, a liar, and a jerk. He was no savior, and he certainly wasn't unique."

Jesus? The Jesus who healed and fed people? Who willingly died in our place for our sins? Who taught us to love our neighbors and to pray for our enemies? That Jesus is a megalomaniacal jerk? Oh wait. Wait. Jesus took authority over unclean spirits and cast them out. Who would hate Jesus like that if not evil spirits?

1 John 4:1 tells us that we can test the spirits by their views of Jesus, the Son of God made flesh. The evil beings that harassed Kyle Odom hated Jesus. It's notable that the first time Kyle attended The Altar, he felt like his life was in danger as soon as he walked in. Simply sitting there made him so uncomfortable that he had to leave. That makes sense for somebody oppressed by unclean spirits, whose fear he sensed as he sat in the midst of people filled with the Holy Spirit.

Tim eventually flew to Boise to visit Kyle Odom in prison. They spoke on several occasions, and Kyle slowly concluded that Tim was not an alien or controlled by the aliens. First, Tim was kind to Kyle and treated him with humanity. Second, the entities stopped harassing Kyle when Tim came around. Kyle also had a reprieve from the entities when his parents visited. They too were Christians.

Tim wasn't angry at Kyle. He prayed for him, that one day he'd find salvation in Jesus the King and be freed from the enemy that sought to destroy him. "I can't wait for the day when he's standing up beside me, giving his testimony." That's the picture in his mind that Tim longed to come true.

"What we have to know is that we have an enemy that singled him out," Tim said. "My perspective? I had this visual of the enemy saying, 'I'm sick to death of that ministry there.' The enemy used Kyle to make a big, bold, grand move, and God said, 'Check Mate.' The whole thing flip-flopped. What the enemy intended for evil, God used for good."

Kyle Odom

Odom arrested in D.C.

Suspect in pastor shooting apprehended in front of the White House

By KEITH COUSINS
Staff Writer

COEUR d'ALENE — Kyle Andrew Odom was arrested by Secret Service agents Tuesday night in front of the White House in Washington, D.C.

Odom, 30, was wanted for the House fence prior to his arrest at 8:27 p.m. EST, Coeur d'Alene Police Chief Lee White said.

"I think we will all sleep a little bit safer tonight," White said. "But our detectives certainly won't be — they've still got a lot of work ahead of them to put together a case that the county

Odom

White

arrest.

Multiple Spokane media outlets, as well as Odom's parents, received identical letters Tuesday morning from the suspected shooter. Inside the envelope was a piece of paper that read "The Truth About Kyle Odom" and a USB drive containing a lengthy manifesto apparently

said. "It's more rambling than anything, there was really no specific 'I'm going to kill this individual' type of threats. We didn't take the names on there lightly, I can tell you that."

Once investigators reviewed the material, and realized the potential scope of whom Odom could target, federal authorities were contacted.

Although he could not state Odom was definitively on Facebook today, White did

'What can I do to help you?'

Pastor still hopes for chance to speak with man accused of shooting him six times

By BRIAN WALKER
Staff Writer

COEUR d'ALENE — Pastor Tim Remington hopes the new year will once and for all bring an opportunity for him to speak with Kyle Odom, who is accused of shooting Remington six times last March.

"What can I do to help you?" Remington said, referring to what he'd say to Odom. "I'd like to help him. I saw him in court, but he never looked at me. I want to meet with him.

"We forgave him after it happened. We're at the

See PASTOR, A4

White said he was told Odom threw computer flash drives and other unidentified items over the White House fence. Hazardous materials and bomb teams were working to identify the other items, he said.

The Secret Service will get first crack at prosecuting Odom for any crimes, Reneau said.

Warrant in attack on pastor didn't stop suspect's flight

Odom's family issued a statement Tuesday evening, saying they were thankful for the safe apprehension of their son.

"As Kyle was not living with us, we are learning of his plans as they are being released by police," Odom's family said. "We are truly thankful to God he is safe and no one else has been injured."

"The deal that we are truly thrilled about is that they caught him without killing him," Johnson said. "I mean, my pastor will be the first guy that will go see him in jail and forgive him for what he did. We just pray for his soul, we really do."

Gun Shot Witness

Credits for news clips on page 53:

Figure 6.3 (Top) - Keith Cousins, "Odom Arrested in D.C.," *Coeur d'Alene Press*, March 9, 2016, https://cdapress.com/news/2016/mar/09/odom-arrested-in-dc-5/

Figure 6.4 (Middle Left) -Brian Walker, "What Can I Do to Help You?" *Coeur d'Alene Press*, December 24, 2016, https://cdapress.com/news/2016/dec/24/what-can-i-do-to-help-you-5/

Figure 6.5 (Middle Right) - Nicholas K. Geranios, "Man Tied to Pastor's Shooting Held in White House Incident," Associated Press in *San Bernardino Sun*, March 10, 2016.

Figure 6.6 (Lower Middle) - Nicholas K. Geranios, "Warrant in Attack on Pastor Didn't Stop Suspect's Flight," Associated Press in *Press-Enterprise* (Riverside, CA), March 8, 2016.

Figure 6.7 (Bottom Left) - "Man Tied to Idaho Shooting Arrested at White House," Associated Press in *Sun Chronicle* (Attleboro, MA), March 10, 2016.

Figure 6.8 (Bottom Right) - Quoting Usher A.J. Johnson in Keith Cousins, "Odom Arrested in D.C.," *Coeur d'Alene Press*, March 9, 2016, https://cdapress.com/news/2016/mar/09/odom-arrested-in-dc-5/

7

THE PUZZLE BALL

Tim believed in spiritual warfare long before Kyle shot him. The Bible describes the planet Earth as a battlefield where demonic powers and holy angels clash in a spiritual realm just beyond the view of our physical eyes. In the days that followed the shooting, Tim had his own experiences with evil spiritual beings, powers that hated him and wanted to destroy him.

Tim regularly slipped in and out of consciousness the first week. Hospital staff had rushed him into surgery as soon as the paramedics brought him in, when Tim's whole body felt like an inferno. After surgery, the intense fiery pain settled into his right arm and back, and even strong pain meds couldn't ease it completely. The place where Tim went when he closed his eyes, though, that proved worse than any physical torment. In the days after the shooting, he found himself drifting back and forth between our physical world and a dark, horrifying space on the balancing edge of life and death.

Tim didn't see light at the end of the tunnel. He didn't see angels or Jesus. When he closed his eyes, he hovered on the brink of eternity, where a dark and malevolent enemy packed the air tight around him. He'd open his eyes and see Cindy beside his bed, and then he'd close his eyes and return to a dark expanse.

"It was like a giant puzzle ball," Tim tried to describe the spiritual reality he experienced. "I was inside a giant ball that appeared to be made of puzzle pieces, all joined together. I couldn't see any light, but once in awhile, a piece of the puzzle would break away from the rest. Light shone through that hole for a moment before it closed up, and then I was back in blackness."

The things that looked like puzzle pieces were sentient beings, and when one or two dropped away from the shell of the ball, they flew at him in the darkness. "I wish I could remember the exact looks that they had. They had knives and sharp spears, and they would fly right at me and then veer away at the last second. I had this Saran Wrap, like a Saran Wrap force field around me. It just blew around, though, wavy and loose, and it seemed like anything could penetrate it."

This was not a fuzzy reality, like a dream. "It was vivid," Tim said. He experienced the full reality of that other place, the place beyond physical eyesight.

Cindy nodded. "Once while I was sitting by his bed, holding his hand, he opened his eyes and looked around, and he said to me, 'You don't see them, do you?'"

Hundreds of beings surrounded Tim, blanketing him in terror. "Two or three at a time would drop away and fly at me, but they were afraid of that light film around me, and they would swerve away at the last moment." Like sharks.

The beings had human forms without human facial expressions. Their flesh stretched back, as though a gusting wind blew the loose skin away from their faces. They flew fast. At first, Tim saw only silhouettes when they dropped down to rush at him, but the details of their bodies became clear as they drew near. They had naked, humanoid bodies, complete with both male and female genitalia, and they took their time to commit perversities in Tim's sight, doing their best to horrify and repulse him. In the interest of decency, Tim offered no details. He simply explained that the males behaved lewdly, and the females exposed themselves in obscene ways.

"Anything they could do to get me into fear, sin, anything, anything they could do." They were pushing Tim hard to discourage him and pummel him psychologically. "I think they were trying to kill me from sheer stress and fear."

Most of the beings had high pitched, squealing voices, but one entity spoke words. Over and over, the same voice threatened him. Even after Tim came home from the hospital, he heard it a few times. It constantly repeated, "I'm going to own you. I'm going to *own* you." Tim answered him, "No. You're not going to own me. I've been bought by the blood of Jesus. You cannot own me!"

When Tim opened his eyes, the light shone and he saw his wife beside him. He wanted to stay with Cindy. He didn't want to close his eyes and return to the darkness of the puzzle ball with those terrible beings.

The doctors didn't know whether Tim would live that first week after the shooting. He teetered there between life and death, drifting into the horror of the puzzle ball and back out into living consciousness. On Sunday, Tim still hung suspended in the darkness, where he waited for another onslaught of spiritual attacks. On and on and on the beings tormented him without mercy. Suddenly, a new voice penetrated Tim's prison of blackness. As he hung in space surrounded by the fluttering film, the gentle voice of Christ spoke to Tim and asked, "Do you want to go Home?"

From the darkness of the puzzle ball, Tim said, "Yes. I want to go Home." As soon as he said it, though, he felt regret and wanted to repent. Tim paused and told the Lord, "I'm sorry. Thirty-five years ago I told You that I was Yours, that You could do whatever with my life that You wanted to. Here I am saying I want to go Home, and if You want me to die, then I'll die, but if You want me to live, then I'll live."

As soon as he said those words, the flimsy Saran Wrap around him ballooned out and got tight, so tight it looked ready to pop. Then, as though Tim were at a concert and somebody had played the lowest note on the synthesizer, the note that shakes the bench, the richest voice in the universe said, "THAT'S ENOUGH."

Those words from Tim's Heavenly Father ended everything. The enemy lost its position; the whole dark puzzle ball disintegrated.

That sphere of darkness crumbled, and as the enemy fled, light washed over Tim.

"As soon as God spoke, that was it. It was over."

Tim opened his eyes and looked around, and he saw only Cindy.

Cindy worked it out, and she believed this was the day that Tim ceased to breathe and the hospital staff jumped in to save his life. From that point onward, Tim improved, and the doctors finally had real confidence that he'd make it. They said, "We don't know what his disabilities are going to be, but we think he's going to survive this."

"Why Saran Wrap, though?" Tim later thought about it, confused. "It sounds dumb, but it was the presence of the Holy Spirit around me, protecting me. It was just so transparent, light and easy, like it was a piece of cake for Him to hold off the attacks of the enemy. That light film literally held everything back."

Despite the darkness of Tim's ordeal, God had constantly, consistently protected him. Satan's forces had clearly focused on Tim Remington for destruction, first by convincing Kyle Odom to shoot him, and then by tormenting him with the intention to finish him off. Neither onslaught succeeded, because God surrounded him. That was encouraging. The very fact that Satan wanted to take Tim out at the knees… that… that was encouraging too. It meant that Tim had been doing work that did damage to Satan's kingdom.

8
CATALDO LIGHTHOUSE

The shooting and survival of Tim Remington raises a significant question that has required investigation: what about Tim made him a prime target? Why did Satan so badly want him dead? North Idaho holds a variety of churches with top-notch, dedicated pastors all fighting serious battles, but Satan zeroed in on Tim Remington in a very visible, public way.

Several years after the shooting, Tim relaxed in an easy chair a few feet from the white piano he was never supposed to play again. He still suffered every day from the mangling of a bundle of nerves in his shoulder. Connections to his right hand had been damaged, and his forearm screamed at him without mercy. Tim had learned to separate himself from it, to disassociate, but sleep still came with difficulty, and he only got a few hours per night. He leaned back in his recliner after a long day and enjoyed a bowl of ice cream, a small pleasure despite the never ending misery in his hand.

The local papers had followed Tim's story, and newspaper clippings about Tim's shooting and recovery filled a scrapbook, along with letters from the state legislature and governor. A blossomed bullet sat on Tim's bookshelf, a flat circle of metal larger than a quarter. It served as a reminder that six of the bullets shot by Kyle Odom had failed to enter their victim. Actually, a

Figure 8.1 - In his living room, Tim Remington holds one of the blossomed .45 bullets that missed him.

seventh bullet did graze Tim's head, but he counted that one as a miss too.

At the request of Congressman Russ Fulcher, a United States flag had been flown over the U.S. Capitol on October 9, 2019 in Tim's honor, and that flag now sat folded in a respectful triangle on Tim's shelf. The whole country had heard about the shooting and survival of Pastor Tim Remington.

Why had Satan focused so keenly on Tim's destruction? What history led ultimately to Kyle Odom's unloading 12 rounds at Tim in his church parking lot?

It certainly started back in southern California, where a shaggy-haired young Tim eventually became assistant pastor at that little white church in San Bernardino, and he and Cindy traveled onto the streets to talk to people about Jesus. It started way back then.

Remember, young Tim hated the fact that most churches

played it safe, keeping inside their comfortable buildings with other Christians. Tim wanted to make sure their church reached outside its walls. He and Cindy helped with the church's coffee house and dojo. They trekked down into the Santa Ana riverbeds, preaching to people or inviting them to the coffee house. They prayed with the intercessory prayer group, and they helped the homeless. Tim took calls for the occult hotline, teaching and praying for people over the phone. He and Cindy took charge of the youth group and worked in the Royal Ranger program for the youngsters. Anything that was going on, Tim and Cindy were involved.

One night at Denny's, Tim discussed salvation with their waitress Cathy, telling her God's plan to save the world through Jesus Christ. Cathy said, "You know, I'm working and I can't talk to you right now. But, I'm going to get off in a little bit. If you wait, we can talk after I get off."

Less than an hour later, Cathy met Tim and Cindy in the parking lot. They told her that God had sent Jesus to die for our sins, that she could be freed from her sins through Him. They prayed with her, and Cathy gave her life to Christ in a real, full, all-heart kind of way.

Not long after that, Tim's faithful dog Bones got a case of heartworms that promised to kill the poor guy. The vet said, "We could give him a blood transfusion, but the heartworms will probably come back." Tim and Cindy didn't have money for the treatment, and they began considering the sad reality that Bones would have to be put down. They didn't want to do it, of course; they postponed euthanizing him, because they didn't want to lose part of their family. The situation grew worse, and soon Bones couldn't stand up. He couldn't keep food down. He was dying, and it became cruel to keep him alive.

One night, Cathy from Denny's came to visit with a group of other young people, and they gathered around Bones and sadly watched the dying dog. Tim and Cindy explained they knew they had to put him down, but he was family. It was hard.

Cathy said, "Have you prayed for him?"

Tim said, "Well, no."

"Let's do it," Cathy said. "Let's pray for him."

This brand new Christian girl knelt there beside Bones and put her hands on him and prayed for him. The young people all gathered around and prayed with her for that loving, faithful dog. The next day, Bones got up and shook his tail as though he'd never been troubled by heartworms a single day of his life. Completely normal, he trotted to his bowl and ate some food. Bones lived for years after that.

God is kind and has so much compassion. Cathy had simple faith in the character of God, in His love and goodness, and the Lord healed Bones right there in the Remington's living room. Tim and Cindy told Cathy about Jesus and Cathy was saved – then Cathy prayed for dear Bones, and Bones was saved. Life begat more life.

That was Tim and Cindy's world. They worked day jobs to pay bills, and they spent the rest of their days and weeks reaching out and ministering to people. Tim hung drywall during the day, and Cindy worked for Mission Aviation Fellowship (MAF), a ministry that flew missionaries to their destinations around the world. The Remingtons continued to do ministry during their spare time week after week, year after year.

Tim's work outside the church walls caught the attention of a man called Sword, a former NASA scientist who claimed to be an antichrist, a god of the underworld. Sword regarded the streets of San Bernardino as his territory. He saw the homeless as his people, and he took care of them, and he didn't want Christians coming into his territory and messing with his people.

"You Christians always come in and then you leave. And these people don't trust you anyway."

Sword didn't come off as a sloppy homeless man, but as an intellectual, a brilliant older gentleman. He used logical arguments to attack the faith of simple people, and he came into the coffee house and spread seeds of doubt even into Cindy's heart. It took

THE PRESS-ENTERPRISE

Former area pastor shot day after Cruz rally

Figure 8.2 - The Riverside, California *Press-Enterprise* remembers its own.

time for her to recover.

During this period, Cindy had one of the few dreams in her life she truly believed came from God. In the dream, she saw Tim as he was, skinny with a blue tank top and canvas bell bottoms, walking down the street with their church behind him. Down the other way on the same street strolled a cranky lion. The lion had large, padded feet, and as Tim walked along, doing what he did, the lion eyed him. When they met, Tim turned to meet him, and they wrestled in the middle of the street. Neither were harmed in the wrestling match. After they wrestled, Tim walked on and the lion shook himself and walked on the other way.

"I believe that Sword was possessed of a bad spirit," Cindy said. "Any spirit who does not claim Jesus is a spirit of antichrist. He blatantly claimed to be an antichrist, and he was one of the scariest people we ever met. Tim has bumped into a lot of people who wanted to kill him, but Sword acted in the power of his lord, and that's what it boils down to. He didn't come in to have a casual conversation. He came in with his sense of authority based on whom he served. It was like tangling with the Devil. If you can walk away from that virtually unscathed, then you've done well."

Spiritual battles were already going on way back then, because Tim kept poking the evil lion that was seeking to devour people in San Bernardino.

Six years into their marriage, Tim and Cindy's first son Jeremiah burst into the world, but a baby boy didn't stop them.

They balanced home life and ministering to the world's hurting people. They dearly loved their church family and all the scattered folks God brought into their lives. Tim served officially as one of the pastors of the church and preached on occasion, but both Tim and Cindy began to feel like God was transitioning them for something else. No single issue moved their hearts, but a variety of different concerns and desires kept pushing them to make a change.

In 1990, Tim received a note that deeply affected him. It warned, "I know where your son goes to preschool," and he knew they had to make a decision. Tim wasn't too bothered when people yelled and cursed and threatened him, but it was completely different to have their child in danger.

"We knew that if we didn't move then, we were in a quandary." They had long wanted to pastor their own church, so it made sense to move. "We wanted to pastor, and we didn't want our kids hurt."

Tim and Cindy made a quick choice to move to North Idaho where Tim's parents lived and find a church needing a pastor. They decided to head north together right away. Right away. They took only the most essential items and left their stuff in the driveway to the guys who worked for them. That was it.

Tim's parents lived up in the hills east of Coeur d'Alene, and Tim and Cindy stayed with them until they were able to buy a little house in town. Tim made a good living hanging drywall, and they'd bought the property right next to his parents years earlier. Eventually, they were able to get a construction loan, and Tim acted as his own contractor. Doing a lot of work themselves, they were able to build the big timber-framed house where Tim later kept a shelf filled with news clippings and a blossomed .45 bullet.

Meanwhile, Tim and Cindy became interim youth pastors at the Assembly of God church in Coeur d'Alene. Tim set up a keyboard in the old sanctuary, and every Monday he'd lead worship and prayer.

Cindy recalled, "We had an all-night prayer meeting for the youth group, and people at the church said, 'The teens are not

Cataldo Lighthouse

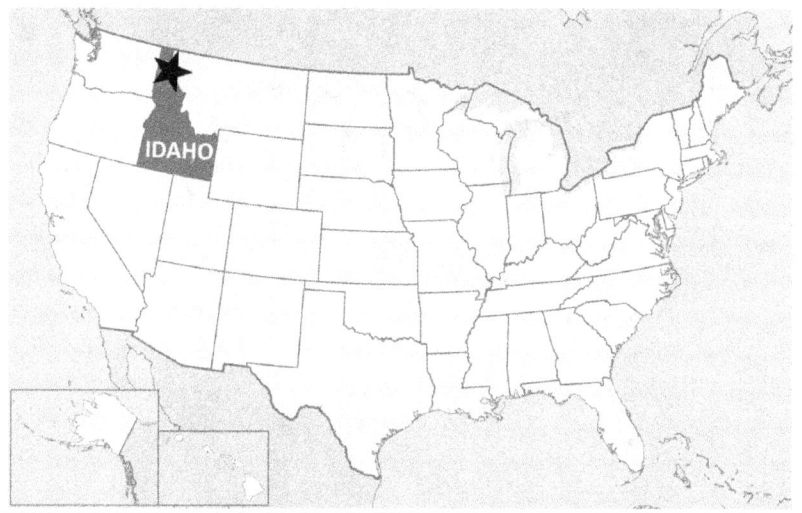

Figure 8.3 - Idaho, the 43rd state. Idaho's Shoshone County is marked by a star.

going to go to an all-night prayer meeting.'"

Kids? Praying for hours and hours? H'yeah right. The teens proved more dedicated than the adults expected, though! They honestly prayed and worshiped into the wee hours, and two of the young men were called to the ministry that night. Both eventually became pastors.

"Amazing things happen when people pray," Cindy said.

Still, Tim felt suspended and unsettled and wanted to do more, so much more. One Sunday, Merle and Glenda Beare attended a Sunday School lesson that Tim was teaching. The Beares had been driving 20 miles over a small mountain pass into Coeur d'Alene for church every week, but they had been praying and praying for God to start a church on the other side of the pass in the Silver Valley. Tim and Cindy caught their attention, so the Beares asked the Remingtons if they'd be interested in starting a new church. Tim felt no draw to Shoshone County, but he decided to drive over the mountain and check it out anyway. He drove up and down the freeway from Cataldo to Wallace and asked God what He thought of the idea.

Tim smiled, "I'll be if I didn't get a love for the Silver Valley."

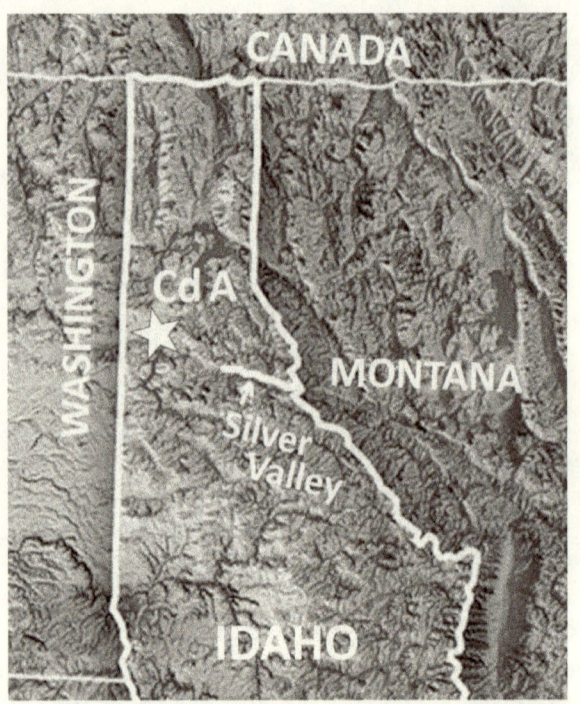

Figure 8.4 - The Silver Valley of N. Idaho is separated from Coeur d'Alene (CdA) by a small mountain pass.

Figure 8.5 - The Bitterroot Range from atop Silver Mountain. The Silver Valley winds through the foothills below.

Cataldo Lighthouse

The city of Coeur d'Alene sits on the shores of a lake that's almost 50 square miles in surface area. It's nestled in a large, open valley between several sets of mountain ranges, and there's plenty of sunshine. It's a beautiful spot in northern Idaho and has become one of the fastest growing areas in the country.

Over Fourth of July Pass to the east, Interstate-90 descends into a narrow valley through the Coeur d'Alene Mountains of the Bitterroot Range, one that winds and bends the 40 miles to Lookout Pass on the Montana Border. That winding gash through the mountains has been called the Silver Valley because more than a billion ounces of silver, along with profitable amounts of lead, zinc and copper have been gouged from its mines since the 1880s. It doesn't sit on a huge, gorgeous lake. It's not open and particularly sunny. The valley runs east and west, but the mountains do their part to block direct sunlight into the gulches and crevices much of the day. The valley offers a history of mining along with alcoholism, drug addiction, prostitution, abuse and violence. There's even a saying in the valley, "If you want to get away with murder, do it in Shoshone County."

Figure 8.6 - The Bunker Hill and Sullivan Mill in Kellogg, Idaho 1904. Note the thinly treed hills. Courtesy Siobhan Ebel, "Silver Mountain Set to Celebrate 50 Years," *Shoshone News-Press*, January 3, 2018.

Shoshone County presented a depressing picture in the 1980s and 90s. The refinery smelter had belched out smoke filled with heavy metals for decades, killing off the vegetation on the mountains around Kellogg, leaving the hillsides barren and ugly. Silver prices dropped in the 1980s and put several of the mines out of business, which drove up unemployment and poverty. After a century of mining, the people of Kellogg were left with an ugly, polluted world and no jobs.

In the late 1980s, the Silver Mountain ski resort built the world's longest gondola up into the mountains above Kellogg, but the first leg of the journey still lifted skiers over a barren, brown land. The nasty orange pool of a mine settling pond lay open below as the gondola carried skiers upward toward the slopes. Over the years, the view improved as new trees slowly refreshed those hills, but little about Kellogg looked pretty in 1993.

Cindy remembered, "It was like coming into a heaviness, a cloud of oppression. There were old strongholds with the prostitution and abuse. There were wonderful people there, but there was this spiritual heaviness. It was known for darkness."

God didn't call Tim and Cindy to Kellogg. Not exactly. He called them to a swampy area some miles to the west of Kellogg. Between the Fourth of July Pass and the Silver Valley sits a wide open marshy area called the Cataldo Slough. As of this writing,

Figure 8.7 - A simple map of the route Interstate 90 takes through northern Idaho east of the city (and lake) of Coeur d'Alene.

Cataldo is pretty enough for a postcard. Farm-dotted hills rise over wetlands filled with reeds and aquatic birds, like a giant, sparkly pond. Cataldo Mission, Idaho's oldest standing building, sits like a white jewel atop one of these hills as a reminder that Catholic missionaries came in the 1840s to serve the local Native American tribe.

It wasn't always lovely, though. In 1975, the Cataldo Slough made a portrait of desolation, mud flats pocked by rusty 55-gallon drums. Cataldo had regained its initial beauty by the time Cindy and Tim decided to take it on, but the area still suffered from the same unemployment and depression and spiritual darkness as the rest of the valley.

The Beares knew they needed a pastor in Cataldo, and they had the confidence to ask Tim to travel over the mountain and pastor a little church that hadn't even started. In faith, the Beares filled out the paperwork to charter the church, and that was the start of Cataldo Lighthouse Ministries.

"There was just a small handful of people, and we decided we were going to go ahead and get the church going," Tim said.

Figure 8.9 - The Cataldo Slough from the northwest.

"But there was no church building. To meet in a person's house would be great, but I knew that we were going to have a problem with that as soon as we started growing, and I was bound and determined that we were going to grow a church.

"I went door-to-door. We literally drew a map of every road that was there, and I was going to mark it off as I went." Like the census man from God. "Door-to-door to every house. It got a little thick when you started to get above Kellogg, but I went from Cataldo to Kellogg, and I tried to hit every house. And we went all the way up Pine Creek and kept moving."

Tim called the local Canyon Elementary School and asked if the church could meet there, and the school agreed. Every week the church members unloaded all the chairs and sound equipment and set them up in the elementary school gym, and then after the service they loaded all the chairs and sound equipment back into a trailer. The school charged the new church just $400 per month, mostly to pay for the electric. As a way to give thanks, the church bought new playground equipment one year, and another year they painted the school.

Figure 8.10 - The Cataldo Mission, Idaho's oldest standing building.

"We were grateful for the Canyon school, and we really tried to give back," Tim said.

It was supposed to be temporary, but Cataldo Lighthouse Ministries ended up spending 12 years at the school, from 1993 until the church moved to Coeur d'Alene in 2005. They filled the gym every Sunday, and people came from as far as Spokane in the west and Montana in the east. They packed in 250-300 people every Sunday - a crazy large congregation for that little town; Cataldo itself hardly had a population of 300, and Canyon Elementary was tucked out of the way.

Satan certainly had his hackles up back then, because that church had all kinds of things going on. On Wednesday nights, church members took up all the seats at the café in Smelterville, between Pinehurst and Kellogg, right beside Johnny's Bar. The Cataldo Lighthouse Fellowship met at the Health and Welfare office in Kellogg for a Bible study and support groups, and 70 people showed up every week. In a county where churches might have 30 people in the pews on Sunday, this was astonishing.

"We'd do anything to get people together," Tim said. "We had the best group of people. It was just lovely. That church grew and grew."

Spiritual warfare took place then as well. The ladies in the church decided to drive up and down the valley and pray. They went to the post offices in each town and stood outside to seek God, because it was a way to pray for everybody in the whole community. They asked God to wash into every house and bless all those people. The next week, a group of men with black hoods, faces shrouded, gathered around the Wallace post office and spiritually tried to take it back. Wallace was famous for its prostitution. It had its history of occultic activity; satanic practices and witchcraft had deep roots in the county. It was a battle.

Despite spiritual struggles, the Cataldo church kept growing. Soon, Tim got on the radio with Roger at the KWAL station for morning devotions. Tim and Roger often joked and teased each other, offering the Silver Valley a bit of morning comedy. Roger and the folks at KWAL gave Tim carte blanche access to their airwaves throughout the day. Tim might randomly call in just for fun banter with Roger, and they'd go after each other for the entertainment of local listeners.

"How's it feel to be so ugly? You've got the best radio face in the business, Roger."

Ironically, Tim first met Roger after Roger's son put a gun to Tim's head.

Tim preached in the Canyon school gym one Sunday about the Bible's warnings against sexual immorality, and a certain 17-year-old kid didn't like that much. He stood in the back and told Tim what he was full of. After the service, Tim and others walked outside, and this young man met them with a 30-06 pointed dead at Tim's face.

"We told him that God loved him, and we loved him. We said, 'Look. You don't want to do this.' We were able to talk him down, and eventually he got saved." The kid's parents became great friends with Tim and Cindy, until Roger and Tim were insulting each other regularly on the radio for the fun of the whole area.

Tim concluded, "We had all kinds of people coming, and we loved them all."

And that was just the beginning.

9
JUSTINE

Among the people who attended the Cataldo church were the parents of Justine Hansen. Justine had struggled for 16 long years addicted to heroin and methamphetamines and had committed crimes she refused to describe out loud, even decades later. By the time Justine turned 31, the misery and failures had dragged her emotionally to the ground, and she couldn't take care of herself, let alone her children. She lived from shelter to shelter and from tents to abandoned houses. Every day offered a new nightmare, and she stumbled along completely broken. She thought, "I can't do this. I can't live like this anymore."

Justine heard from her parents that their new church helped drug addicts. They had become friends with Tim and Cindy and encouraged her that Tim would help her, so Justine took a chance. She called Pastor Tim, and rather than putting Justine in yet another shelter, Tim and Cindy invited her into their home and let her sleep on their couch for several days. "I remember being so grateful for a safe, warm place to sleep."

Justine didn't simply need a home, though. She needed freedom from her addictions. She needed a new shot at life. After four days of sleeping at the Remington house, Tim put Justine on a plane to southern California, to a faith-based drug rehab facility called Calvary Ranch. During the month-long program, the love of God overwhelmed Justine. She finally understood in a real way the truth that Jesus Christ laid down His life so that she could have a brand new life.

That changed everything for Justine. She gave all her crud to God, all her addictions and crimes and sins were surrendered to the Lord, and she told God her life belonged to Him.

The world is overwhelmed with dead churches filled with people trying to be "good," and the world's hurting souls look at those empty, guilt-filled places and hate them. Nobody wants that. There's a common idea that people have to clean themselves up in order to become Christians, but if that were the case, all of humanity would be doomed, stuck up to its chin in its own fetid quicksand, gagging from the stench and preparing to drown. The incredible reality is that God takes broken people filled with shame, and He sets them free. He breaks their chains. He cleans them up and makes them capable of serving Him. That's the only way it can work.

Where the Spirit of the Lord is, there's freedom, and when Justine surrendered herself to God, He showed her something precious. He promised He would redeem the past 31 years of her life and use all that destruction for good.

Justine explained her own rebirth at Calvary Ranch. "During those 31 days, the Spirit of God that raised Jesus from the dead came into my life and literally raised me from the dead. He healed me and made me a new person. I was completely transformed."

The Remingtons didn't drop Justine after that. When she returned to Idaho, Tim and Cindy invited her to live in their home for the next eight months, giving her time to grow strong. They mentored her and helped her build her knowledge of the Bible.

"That time at their home was a blessing, and I am eternally grateful for all the love they've shown me."

God redeemed Justine's first three decades as He promised He would. All those months Justine stayed in his home, Tim had been dreaming and planning about starting a drug rehab facility there in North Idaho. It was good to send people down to Calvary Ranch, but it was better to have a refuge right there in Coeur d'Alene, their own Good Samaritan Rehabilitation. When Tim and Cindy opened their first facility, Tim asked Justine if she would run it.

The idea terrified Justine. She didn't feel ready to run a drug rehab house, and she didn't particularly relish the thought of living with a bunch of women!

"Lord," she asked. "What do you want me to do?"

In answer, the Lord directed her to 1 Corinthians 1:27:

But God hath chosen the foolish things of the world to confound the wise; and God hath chosen the weak things of the world to confound the things which are mighty;

Justine's lack of self-confidence meant little, because God would equip her and qualify her for the job He'd given her. God was able to rescue a foolish young woman, who'd spent so much of her adult life in and out of shelters, addicted and troubled, and He'd use her to bless other women.

By 2016 when Tim was shot, Justine had developed into a mother figure for hundreds of former drug addicts. Silver haired and full cheeked, with warm brown eyes behind her glasses, the old needle scars up and down her arms didn't match the rest of her. They didn't fit the happy, loving woman who mentored multitudes of hurting women. Nobody who met Justine on the street would guess she'd spent 16 years of her life controlled by drugs.

Luke 12:48 tells us that much is required of those who have received much. The Lord had blessed Justine with the world - forgiveness and freedom and a loving new family - and Justine longed to give her life back to God by caring for others.

The first home, The Ranch, opened on January 1st, 2003 as a woman's rehabilitation facility. In the years after, Good Samaritan Rehabilitation also opened three men's facilities, and Justine remained the assistant director over the whole program. Each facility was a house, an actual house with bedrooms and a kitchen and dining room where everybody ate together as a family.

The houses had yards, and the men's houses included workout rooms with weights and garages with tools to build things. House members might leave to go to church or volunteer or do crafts.

The program that Tim and Justine developed was not easy. It was a regimented program, and each part had a purpose. The clients were not at summer camp; they were there to address the deep issues of their lives, to deal with the reasons they had turned to drugs in the first place. They were there to learn the Bible and get filled with the Word of God. God was there with them, and He did the real work. The houses became places of refuge and healing where people suffering from severe addictions could find the support needed to start their lives brand new and whole.

"I knew I was being called," Justine finished her story. "I had the feeling that if I said, 'No,' I'd probably be swallowed by a fish of some sort." She agreed to take on the new adventure that God had provided for her, and that adventure led to freedom for the hundreds and hundreds of others who came after, even some among her old drug buddies – like Angel Bingham.

10
ANGEL

The world is small, and the underworld is even smaller. Tim started to draw out a tree that connected folks who came to the church with the people from their old lives. Angel Bingham popped up in a lot of trees as the dealer for many of the addicts who walked through Tim's church doors.

Angel grew up in the biker gang world, right behind the clubhouse for the Gypsy Jokers. She started selling pot and acid at age 12 and soon graduated to harder drugs. Opiates became her specialty, but Angel sold everything. The work came naturally to her, and she was good at it.

Tim knew Angel. He repeatedly went to court to offer her the program, but Angel always chose jail instead. When she was released, she thanked Tim by going to church for the simple fun of causing trouble. She interrupted him. She asked hostile questions. She challenged God and the Bible, and nothing Tim said seemed to make a difference.

Eventually, Angel decided to try God for real. She attended Candlelight Christian Fellowship in Coeur d'Alene and sang during worship time. She felt movement in her heart, but she'd light up after service and continue her life on and off drugs with her husband.

The final time she got busted, Angel faced real trouble. Her multiple felonies – possession, selling, burglary, grand theft – meant prison for the rest of her life, and she needed a way out.

After all that, Tim hadn't given up on her. He offered her the program one more time, and this time Angel took it.

Of course, living in a house with a bunch of women focused on Jesus and the Bible was completely weird to Angel. People kept giving her hugs and telling her they loved her? That was not her thing at all. Then, a house leader came to her one day and said, "I'm so sorry to tell you this, but your husband has gotten together with another woman."

Angel's heart broke. She had never been much of a crier, but that night Angel crawled into her bed and curled up by herself. The overwhelming rejection and aloneness dripped into her ears while the house hung silent around her. She rolled over and pressed her damp face into the pillow, and that's when it was like God Himself showed up in her room. He had always felt so far away, so distant, and now He came close beside her and gave her His comfort. Her husband had abandoned her, but God hadn't. For the first time in her life Angel felt God's love, and she finally gave in.

"Okay, God. I'm done. Uncle."

There was no sinner's prayer, no altar call. Angel simply surrendered her life to the King of the universe, and the next morning she awoke with the burning of the Holy Spirit in her chest. She didn't understand that fire, but Angel understood God had saved her and filled her, and it changed everything.

Like her old drug pal Justine, life and health filled Angel's face as the Lord healed her from years of drug abuse. By 2016, silver threads graced Angel's long, dark hair, but life and amused joy radiated from her face as she told her story. Nobody would have guessed she'd grown up on drugs; she looked like the sort of person who should serve on staff at The Ranch. Which is exactly where God brought her. After years of her own self-destruction, God had performed the great miracle and developed Angel into a mentor, a solid, mature woman ready to love on the troubled young ladies who walked through those doors.

No wonder Satan wanted to destroy Tim – and he didn't give up just because Tim survived the shooting.

11

PERFORATIONS

God had clearly saved Tim's life, and the doctors, news outlets, and general public recognized it. However, that didn't mean Tim floated along on clouds post-shooting. Healing took a long, difficult time.

Dropping everything else, missing work, Tim's kids came and sat with him constantly, day after day. They had to sit quietly, which wasn't easy for any of the Remingtons. When the medical staff finally removed his respirator, Tim was able to joke a little, and that encouraged everybody.

Jeremiah showed Tim the picture that Kyle Odom had drawn, the one that portrayed Tim as an alien, and they were able to laugh about it. At that point, the whole family felt relieved, because it finally felt like Dad would be okay. They had their father back.

From the day of the shooting, Jeremiah had stepped into the role of family leader. He checked with the associate pastors as they took charge during Tim's absence. He acted as the family liaison to the press, keeping the local news outlets up-to-date on Tim's progress. He had a family of his own, but Jeremiah took turns sitting with his father, and he made it clear from the start that the family wanted to forgive Kyle Odom and were praying for his spiritual freedom.

Tim couldn't take any simple action for granted, though. Things that had once been easy now rose up as massive walls to climb. Breathing. Sitting up. Bathing. After days and days of lying in bed, feeling sponged and gross, Tim longed for a real shower.

Coeur d'Alene is a relatively calm town, the sort of place where shootings are uncommon. Kootenai Medical Center rarely saw gunshot victims, not ones that survived anyway, and they were reluctant to let their patient bathe under a stream of water. The hospital staff felt insufficient to protect all those deep, raw wounds in a shower, and they didn't want to risk infections that would rage through Tim's whole system. Tim certainly couldn't sneak into the hospital bathroom on his own.

A new young woman, a nurse's aide, came in to care for Tim. She entered the room with enthusiasm before she'd learned anything about the patient, and Cindy and Josiah jumped to stop her as she prepared to take hold of the damaged man in the bed. The family had gotten really good at protecting Tim from dangerous good intentions.

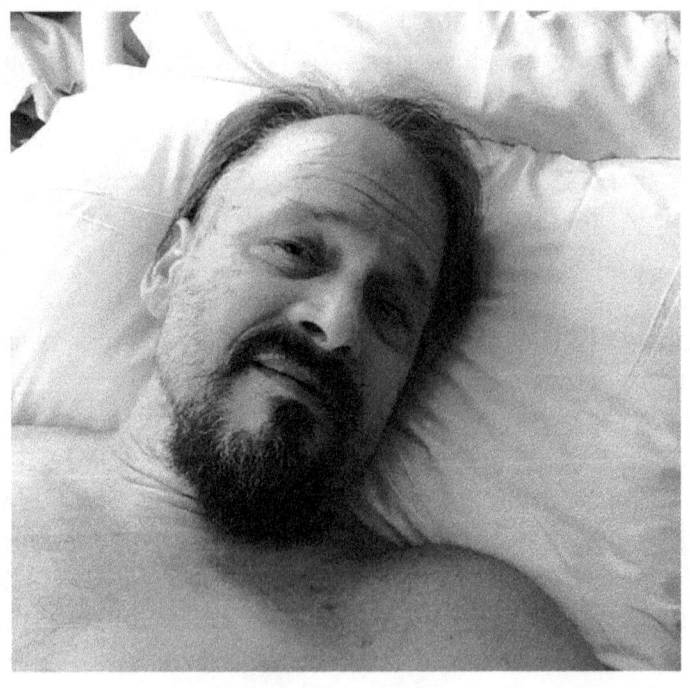

Figure 11.1 - Tim, happier off the hated respirator. Photo by Julie Geist.

Josiah felt deeply that he'd been inaccessible four hours away when his dad was attacked. He remained by his father's bedside day after day, serving as Tim's protector - and Tim needed a constant guard. Every new shift of nurses and physical therapists entered to do their jobs, unaware of the incredible trauma Tim's body had experienced. Tim needed the constant shield of his family, and Josiah took his turns seriously.

Josiah reached out to halt the nurse and said, "You don't want to do that. He got shot."

The nurse laughed and said, "That's funny. What's he really in for?"

"No no," said Josiah. "You need to look at his chart. He got shot."

The young woman hadn't expected that. "Really? He got shot?" Compassionate, she turned to Tim and asked, "Okay. What *can* I do for you?"

Tim said honestly, "What I'd really love is a shower. I haven't been able to take a shower."

Young, energetic, willing to do whatever she could, that young lady took care of it. She left for awhile, and when she came back, she asked, "Do you still want that shower?"

"Yessss," Tim said.

"Okay, we'll get you a shower."

The next time she returned, she brought plastic bags and duct tape, like a hit man, and she covered up every one of Tim's wounds. Tim and Cindy felt certain she was breaking some rules, but the aide did it anyway. She carefully helped Tim into a wheelchair and rolled him into the bathroom.

Cindy got into the shower with Tim as the spraying water drenched her clothes. The holes in Tim's body left him a big mess, and he had no energy. He leaned over and passed out against Cindy's chest as she held him, and she had to catch him and call the nurse. But to bathe under running water? Oh! Tim is forever grateful to that young woman for having mercy and helping him enjoy an honest-to-goodness wash.

After 11 days in the ICU, they moved Tim to the hospital's general population. Things were looking up, and the whole family felt excited. He was out of intensive care! The worst was over! Amidst all the improvements, a nagging pain in Tim's gut seemed unimportant, but he mentioned it to surgeon Dr. Timothy Quinn because it kept bugging him.

The day of the shooting, Dr. Holman had looked at scans of Tim's insides, and he'd seen what looked like a bit of bruising on his colon from one of the bullets. When Tim complained about his tummy 11 days later, Dr. Quinn decided to take another set of scans. This time, he saw that the weak spot on Tim's colon had broken open into a legitimate perforation. This was serious, because it meant leaking. It meant infection.

Two hours after Tim had been moved to gen pop, two hours after rejoicing over all their victories, Dr. Quinn rushed the injured man back into surgery to repair his colon. A nurse told the family, "If another half-hour had passed before Dr. Quinn caught that, you might have lost him."

The enemy hadn't given up its efforts to end her husband, and Cindy realized they still needed to pray for Tim's protection and recovery. Jadon and Gracie were in the waiting room with Cindy when she learned Tim would return to the ICU after surgery. "Will you guys pray with me for your dad?" she asked her children. "We need to be praying. We need to do spiritual warfare."

Spiritual warfare meant reconnaissance. It meant creating a defensive position before settling in, so they went up to the ICU to find out what room he'd be in. "Can we go in there?" Cindy asked.

"We don't normally do that," the nurse said.

"We just want to pray."

The nurse relented and led them into a corner room. She drew the curtains around for them, and Jadon and Gracie and Cindy sought God's protection in advance of Tim's return to the ICU. They prayed that the Lord would rebuke the enemy and keep him completely out of the area.

"That's one of the sweet moments in all that time," Cindy remembered. "I opened my eyes, and I had one kid, Jadon, with his arms up in the air, and Gracie down on the floor just praying. Both of them oblivious to anybody and anything, worshiping, praying for their dad. There were half a dozen special moments during that time, and that was one of those moments. To see my children interceding for their dad like that is something I will carry in my heart forever. It was just beautiful."

Tim needed that intercession, because he had some deeply discouraging realities to face when he woke up. During all that ordeal, the first time Cindy actually saw Tim angry was when he woke up and realized they'd put him back on the respirator. The hated respirator. To add even more frustration, Dr. Quinn gave Tim a temporary colostomy with a colostomy bag that had to be regularly cleaned. After his colon had healed, Dr. Quinn was able to reverse the colostomy, but it added one more thing to the list of issues that kept Tim from normal life.

Tim had been shot! He'd been shot six times and had eight holes in him! God had saved his life, but he had a multitude of issues to work through, not to mention the weakness and pain. Healing from all those injuries took time!

"You couldn't touch him," Cindy said. "You couldn't touch his right arm. Just a touch, and the pain would send him through the roof. His brachial plexus had been damaged. We all know that if you have a little nerve pain – in your mouth or in your back – you can barely move. It stops you in your tracks. Well, you have this whole nerve cluster in your brachial plexus, in your shoulder, and his kept firing and misfiring."

Tim's brain was trying to make sense of the neural chaos, wrestling to translate these strange messages from his damaged nerves, and the resulting pain manifested in different ways in his right arm.

Tim slept in a bed in the living room when they first brought him home. One day, he looked over at Cindy and in shocked accusation asked, "Why did you do that?"

"What are you talking about?" Cindy said.

"Why would you bend my fingers back like that?"

"Dear, I would never do that. I would never bend your fingers back."

Tim puzzled at Cindy as she sat with her hands in her lap. "You didn't touch me, did you?"

"No, I didn't touch you."

In trying to understand the misfiring nerves, Tim's brain interpreted one message as though somebody had grabbed his hand and wrenched his fingers over backward to his wrist. His brain constantly tried to translate the jumbled information from that damaged bundle of nerves in his shoulder.

Dr. Quinn had caught the perforated colon in time, and that saved Tim's life, but there were other dangers in his future, other emergencies to overcome. It was important that people kept praying without giving up, because the Destroyer still had murderous intentions on Tim's life.

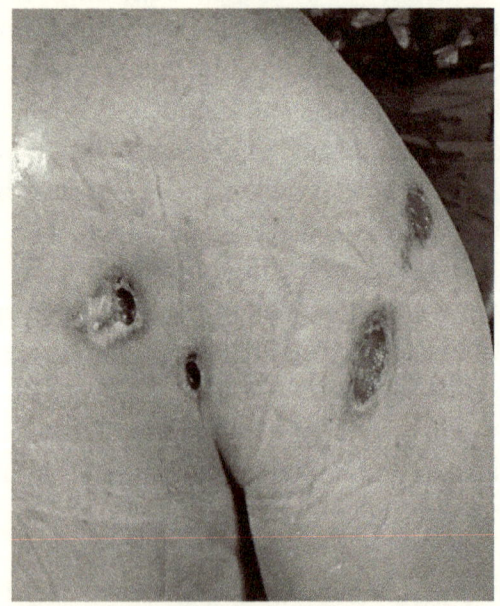

Figure 11.2 - The holes in Tim's shoulder and arm.
Photo by Julie Geist.

12
HOMEWARD BOUND

Tim wanted to go home. After 19 days in the hospital, he didn't care anymore. He just wanted to go home.

"All you're doing is monitoring me," Tim insisted.

A tough and no-nonsense head nurse listened to Tim and thought about it. Finally, she pushed a loose lock of brunette hair behind her ear and said, "Actually, if Cindy can learn to do the things you need, you can go home." That petite, brave woman helped them. She always got straight to the point, but she impressed Tim and Cindy with how she went out of her way to be kind.

Associate Pastor Kurt Neely offered the use of his small transporter bus with a wheelchair lift. They eased Tim gently into a wheelchair and bundled him up with blankets and pillows for padding, then wheeled him through the hospital and onto the lift of Kurt's van. All four of the kids walked their dad down the hall to the van - a little Remington parade. The lift whirred as it raised him up, and they rolled him in.

Despite all their care, each jostle grieved Tim's weak and torn body. No matter how well they bundled pillows around him, the bumps in the road tormented him as Kurt drove him home. They had to lower him again and carefully, so carefully, roll him up the front steps and into the living room where a bed had been made up for him.

That lovely, no-nonsense nurse made visits to their home to make sure Tim had everything he needed, and Cindy provided all the care the nurses had given Tim at the hospital – and more.

blockage while in the hospital. He was no longer on blood thinners after he went home - an oversight on somebody's part - and the weakness on his left side had been caused by a small stroke.

Even more important, the doctors discovered a major infection in Tim's abdomen. Dr. Quinn sewed up his colon and cleaned up the site, but plenty of matter had leaked out before the perforation was discovered. Sally hadn't dismissed Tim's slight fever, and that saved his life. Again.

The stroke and infection seemed to explain everything, but one particular ER doctor felt certain something was being overlooked. In fact, it kept him up all night. "There's something else there. I know there's something else there," he told himself. The next morning, he rushed in and had Tim sent for a chest X-ray, and that's when they found a giant saddle clot. Because he'd spent so much time lying on his back, the blood had pooled and a massive pulmonary embolism had developed in Tim's chest.

A saddle pulmonary embolism is a clot stuck in the Y where the main pulmonary artery branches off to the right and left lungs. It's a serious, life-threatening condition, because it can inhibit the flow of blood into the lungs and through the heart out to the rest of the body. It's a potential death sentence.

"What do we do about that?" Cindy asked the doctor.

"Well… he's doing it," the doctor said. "Normally, he'd be in the ICU for another 12 days, fighting for his life while we tried to dissolve the thing, but for some reason his body is accommodating it."

The doctors never removed the saddle clot; they let Tim's body continue to do its thing without harassing him more. However, they wanted to keep Tim in the hospital on the IV in order to provide a continual regiment of antibiotics and ensure no more clots caused problems. Every four hours his IV bag needed to be changed and reloaded. Tim loathed being back in the hospital and asked if there was any way he could go home.

"Please," he asked. "Please. If we can get the necessary

12

HOMEWARD BOUND

Tim wanted to go home. After 19 days in the hospital, he didn't care anymore. He just wanted to go home.

"All you're doing is monitoring me," Tim insisted.

A tough and no-nonsense head nurse listened to Tim and thought about it. Finally, she pushed a loose lock of brunette hair behind her ear and said, "Actually, if Cindy can learn to do the things you need, you can go home." That petite, brave woman helped them. She always got straight to the point, but she impressed Tim and Cindy with how she went out of her way to be kind.

Associate Pastor Kurt Neely offered the use of his small transporter bus with a wheelchair lift. They eased Tim gently into a wheelchair and bundled him up with blankets and pillows for padding, then wheeled him through the hospital and onto the lift of Kurt's van. All four of the kids walked their dad down the hall to the van - a little Remington parade. The lift whirred as it raised him up, and they rolled him in.

Despite all their care, each jostle grieved Tim's weak and torn body. No matter how well they bundled pillows around him, the bumps in the road tormented him as Kurt drove him home. They had to lower him again and carefully, so carefully, roll him up the front steps and into the living room where a bed had been made up for him.

That lovely, no-nonsense nurse made visits to their home to make sure Tim had everything he needed, and Cindy provided all the care the nurses had given Tim at the hospital – and more.

She learned to clean and replace his colostomy bag. She patiently waited on him and worked to keep him comfortable.

Still. The pain pushed on and on. Tim didn't want to depend on pain medications and live out his days as a drugged up vegetable, because that's what it would have taken to fully deaden the horrible burning in his right arm.

Ice. Packs of ice. Cindy piled them around Tim's burning limb there in his bed in the living room. The ice worked to numb his arm, to ease the misery long enough for him to drift off and enter the land of deep sleep. Down, deep down, into dreams without memory, merciful unconsciousness and peace, if only for a few hours.

"It was amazing how God sustained us through those months."

While awake, Tim rested or listened to music, but he couldn't walk and his right arm remained cradled, limp and useless. Twice a week, Sally the home healthcare worker came into the house to look after Tim's health. She checked his vitals. She made sure he was stable. Cindy changed his bandages, but it was Sally who tenderly fed gauze into Tim's deep wounds.

Cindy watched the treatment of those caverns in awed amazement. "The nurses had a special gauze that they would thread into Tim's wounds to soak up stuff, and they'd pack and pack it in, and then later, they'd pull and pull and pull it out. They were holes! He had holes in him!"

Meanwhile, Tim needed to work his muscles. The physical therapist started her visits to the Remington house right away. She told him, "You have to start moving, Tim. You have to start stretching. You have to start bending."

Stretch? Bend? Tim couldn't feel his leg. He couldn't feel his arm. His white piano waited for him across the living room, silent and a little dusty. Tim wondered how he would ever play it again. He could drag his right arm across the table, if he had something soft to drag it on, but every movement took great effort.

Dr. Linthicum made a house call and told the Remingtons they had to start touching Tim's arm again. The injured man lived in daily suffering, but Dr. Linthicum warned that they needed to go the hard route and desensitize his arm through physical contact.

"Take a wash rag and gently wipe over it," Dr. Linthicum said. If they didn't go through this process, Tim's arm would remain so sensitive that every breeze would agonize him, and eventually they'd have to remove the limb altogether.

Kevin Sgroi from Joshua Tree Physical Therapy also warned Tim to let people touch his arm and get it used to physical contact. He hooked up a machine that shocked Tim's hand and arm to stimulate the nerves. They needed to get the nerves in that arm to calm down.

Tim started with rubber bands - stretching, stretching, using muscles. His right side was still useless, but he could work the muscles on his left side - until the morning Tim awoke to find that his whole left side had lost its strength as well.

"Dear, I think something's wrong," Tim told Cindy. "My whole left side is weak."

"You've been using the rubber bands. Maybe you just overworked yourself," Cindy suggested. She called Sally, who came and checked Tim over.

"Hmm," Sally said. "If it were just the weakness, I'd probably say we should wait it out. But, he also has a slight fever. I think we should send him back to the hospital."

Kurt returned with his van, and they packed Tim up with blankets and pillows as carefully as they could. Then, jostle jostle jostle, Tim returned to the emergency room. Which was awful. The whole experience of entering the ER caused Tim emotional trauma; wheeling through those doors replayed the horror over again.

But praise God that Sally had the sense to send Tim back! All those healing wounds clearly threatened to produce blood clots, clots that might break free and float through his circulatory system and block blood flow. Tim had been on blood thinners to prevent a blockage while in the hospital. He was no longer on blood thinners after he went home - an oversight on somebody's part - and the weakness on his left side had been caused by a small stroke.

Even more important, the doctors discovered a major infection in Tim's abdomen. Dr. Quinn sewed up his colon and cleaned up the site, but plenty of matter had leaked out before the perforation was discovered. Sally hadn't dismissed Tim's slight fever, and that saved his life. Again.

The stroke and infection seemed to explain everything, but one particular ER doctor felt certain something was being overlooked. In fact, it kept him up all night. "There's something else there. I know there's something else there," he told himself. The next morning, he rushed in and had Tim sent for a chest X-ray, and that's when they found a giant saddle clot. Because he'd spent so much time lying on his back, the blood had pooled and a massive pulmonary embolism had developed in Tim's chest.

A saddle pulmonary embolism is a clot stuck in the Y where the main pulmonary artery branches off to the right and left lungs. It's a serious, life-threatening condition, because it can inhibit the flow of blood into the lungs and through the heart out to the rest of the body. It's a potential death sentence.

"What do we do about that?" Cindy asked the doctor.

"Well… he's doing it," the doctor said. "Normally, he'd be in the ICU for another 12 days, fighting for his life while we tried to dissolve the thing, but for some reason his body is accommodating it."

The doctors never removed the saddle clot; they let Tim's body continue to do its thing without harassing him more. However, they wanted to keep Tim in the hospital on the IV in order to provide a continual regiment of antibiotics and ensure no more clots caused problems. Every four hours his IV bag needed to be changed and reloaded. Tim loathed being back in the hospital and asked if there was any way he could go home.

"Please," he asked. "Please. If we can get the necessary

Homeward Bound

equipment and Cindy can learn to use it, can I go home?"

That faithful, no-nonsense head nurse agreed to help them again, and Tim was able to return - jostle jostle jostle - back to his house via Kurt Neely's van. Cindy got up in the middle of the night to change Tim's IV bag. She cleaned his tubes and colostomy bags and looked after him, getting snatches of sleep when she could.

Beyond the ongoing threats to his life and the constant physical pain, his injuries humbled Tim. Not long after his colon surgery, the family rolled Tim into the local Denny's. He'd always enjoyed this Denny's; he'd often brought clients there to eat and talk before moving them into a rehab house. Now, Tim returned to the familiarity of his favorite restaurant shamefully conscious of his brokenness. He sat at a table in a wheelchair with a colostomy bag at his side. Cindy had to feed him, and he had to take a pill so the food wouldn't upset his stomach and come right back up again. He felt less than a man and started feeling sorry for himself, and Tim went straight to bed in discouragement when they got home.

"Tim, look at you," he said to himself. "How are you going to preach if you can't even get out of a wheelchair?"

With that question, a passage from the Bible bumped into his thoughts. In Acts 14, the Apostle Paul was stoned after preaching in the town of Lystra. Those stones were not pebbles; being stoned meant big gashes and broken bones and a smashed skull. The people left Paul in a crumpled heap on the ground outside the city, presumed dead. Sometime later, he rose up again by the power of the Lord. Acts 14:20 tells us that Paul not only survived, he turned and walked back into the city where he'd been attacked. He didn't run away; he faced the very people who'd just attempted to murder him.

"Can you imagine being one of the guys who hit him in the head with a rock?" Tim said. "Can you imagine that? Seeing Paul walk right back in?"

Tim didn't witness Paul's recovery outside the gates of Lystra. He also didn't witness what happened in a Judean grave on Resurrection Sunday two millennia ago, but he had seen the power of God to transform people *because* Jesus Christ rose from the dead. Tim had seen God working firsthand, and he knew God could still work in him. His wounded body would not stump the God of the universe. Tim was broken. He couldn't even feed himself, but it wasn't his own power that would give him the ability to preach and teach again.

"Tim," he said to himself. "You have to stop feeling sorry for yourself. You're not an invalid. You are more than a conqueror. You are an overcomer, and you will overcome."

Six months after the shooting, the two bullets in Tim's shoulder started to surface. He had to go back in so the doctors could make incisions and pull them out. Before the procedure, though, Tim started having some chest pains. Of course, the doctors didn't want to take any chances: they rushed him in for a chest X-ray. After examining the pictures, a doctor said, "Pastor Remington… the blood clot is gone." The dangerous saddle clot in his pulmonary artery had disappeared.

Tim believes the Lord chose to remove the saddle clot in that moment, and he'd felt it in those temporary chest pains.

Of course, the two surfacing bullets had more than sentimental value. They were needed as evidence in the trial against Kyle Odom, and officers stood in the operating room to collect the bullets in a brown evidence bag as soon as the doctors plucked them out. Cindy and Tim wanted to see the bullets before they were tucked away in some evidence locker at the police station, but the officers had to take the bullets as protocol.

The officers understood, though. They slipped out of the operating room, and from the hall they beckoned to Cindy in the waiting room. "Hey. We can let you see them." Cindy followed them into the hallway, where they showed her a piece of rounded metal bigger than a quarter. That flattened bullet with scalloped edges had worked its way through Tim's back to the top of his shoulder? Seven inches, from its entry to his shoulder? For the first time, Cindy appreciated how huge those bullets were, like burning jagged Frisbees through her husband's flesh. Tim had survived them.

The miracle of it struck Cindy, and she thought about the multitude of shrapnel shards stuck inside Tim. Any one of them could be wiggling its way through him. His body's defense system might encapsulate all those shards in scar tissue and keep them protected forever, or it might try to shove them out! So many pieces of metal. So much damage.

God had protected Tim this far, though. No weapon formed against him had prospered, and it looked like God had Tim signed up for the long game.

Remington walks with his 1-year-old granddaughter, Lily, in his driveway on Tuesday.

Figure 12.1 - Credit: Photo by Kathy Plonka, featured in Scott Maben, "Pastor Shot 6 Times Returns to Church," *The Spokesman-Review* (Spokane, WA), June 5, 2016.

Figure 13.1a, b - Credit: Mike Patrick, "Pastor Tim: Always Going After 'Misfits,'" *Coeur d'Alene Press*, March 7, 2016, https://cdapress.com/news/2016/mar/07/pastor-tim-always-going-after-misfits-5/.

13
FLOODS AND DRUGS

The Coeur d'Alene River runs through the eastern part of the Idaho panhandle, down through the Chain Lakes into Coeur d'Alene Lake, and the Spokane River runs out the other side and onward down through Spokane, Washington. It's a land of beautiful lakes, full of fishing and boating and water skiing every summer. In the spring, the rivers swell with melting snow, sometimes to dangerous levels. The flood level of the Coeur d'Alene River near Cataldo is 43 feet, and in 1996 it overflowed to 51.6 feet – almost nine feet above its banks.[1] Some church members lost everything in the flood's ferocity. Water washed through to the ceiling in Mrs. Donna Nelson's home and the whole thing was a loss. According to a February 11, 1996 article in the *Idaho Statesmen,* the panhandle was a "sodden landscape of blown-out highways, wrecked homes, rock slides and mud."[2]

The church jumped at a chance to serve the community. A variety of church members dove into helping those whose houses had been flooded, cleaning and drying and repairing damaged homes. The gusto and visible love of Christ working in that tragedy brought even more people into the church. People got saved, and they filled all the chairs that little Jeremiah helped set

---

1 "Floods," Idaho Office of Emergency Management, https://ioem.idaho.gov/news/a-history-of-idaho-disasters/floods/
2 Ibid.

up every Sunday.

The flood offered another exciting opportunity for Tim and some brave church members: a rafting trip down the Spokane River as its waters swelled.

"It was cold and fast," Tim grinned.

A reporter from a local television station filmed just as Tim's raft slid down into the notorious Devil's Toenail. The Devil's Toenail is tricky to navigate even when the river isn't raging to the lip, and Tim and company were plain foolish to try it during the spring flood season. The reporter's video followed their raft as it bent around the corner and then – boom – disappeared. It was just gone. The flood had raised the water 12 feet higher in that spot, and the raft dropped right out of sight. Even over the roaring of the river, the sound of screaming could be heard on the video.

"It was me hanging onto the side," Tim admitted. "My legs were like clamps on the side of the raft." The others were rowing and rowing, trying to keep out of the hole so they didn't get sucked back into it. "So, I'm screaming. And I'm the only one - the only one on the side of the raft."

Tim kept hollering, "Dig! Dig!" The fellow piloting the thing flew foward, while Roger from the radio station clung to the ropes on the front of the raft.

"It was crazy, and that's why they showed it on the news. Everybody thought we were so stupid. Which we were."

God led wild and crazy Tim Remington and his family into a depressed land, and it seems they were just what the valley needed. Tim was nuts enough to make a difference. The Silver Valley surged with hurting people, just as the Coeur d'Alene River surged with water every spring.

In 2003, Tim and Justine started the woman's rehab facility "The Ranch" in Tim's parents' old home next to the one he and Cindy built. Next, they worked on growing the men's facilities. The men's program lasted 60 days, but the clients then needed transition homes for support while they found jobs and saved the money they needed to live independently. Tim and Justine found

Floods and Drugs

that women needed more time to unpack emotional luggage, so the women's program was 120 days of intensive care before moving on to a transition home. The Remingtons opened their house to provide months of support in that second phase of the rehabilitation program, and other church members followed them. Over the years, Tim and Cindy mentored more than 600 people in their house, all while their kids were growing up. Addicts aren't people known for their trustworthiness, but Tim and Cindy depended on God to protect them all. They enjoyed the people, and they enjoyed watching God transform one person after another after another.

It wasn't about religion or joining a church group. It was about people being healed through encounters with the living God who loved them.

Tess

Tess smoked meth for the first time at eleven years old – with her mother. When she was 13, her dad traded her to a 35-year-old man for drugs.

"How do you ever have a functional, normal life when that's the kind of childhood you had?" Tim remembered young Tess.

Christ got ahold of Tess, and over the years that damaged girl healed as she walked with the Lord. She eventually married a man she loved and had children, and nobody would guess at the destruction in her early life.

Steve

Steve was born to a 15-year-old mother and 19-year-old father, both addicts. He grew up angry and uncontrollable, and while in juvenile detention he learned his mother was found hung to death in a tree. Jail became Steve's comfort zone, and as an adult he'd commit crimes just to be sent back.

Steve noticed that people kept leaving the drug culture because they were going to church. On one of his trips to court, the public defender told him he had the option to attend the Good Samaritan

Program. In fact, two of Steve's former drug buddies were his sponsors. On May 6th, 2012, at the age of 26, Steve surrendered his life to the Lord and went on to become a pastor himself, learning to lay down his life and serve people like Jesus had done. He loved to minister to the young men, the street kids and addicts who came through the church. He married a Christian woman, and one of the biggest blessings in Steve's life was to give his children the dad and family he never had.

Cara

Cara battled with anorexia from early childhood and began to self-harm in high school. Mental health specialists provided her with a long list of psychiatric diagnoses. She wasn't stupid - that wasn't her problem; she earned a 4.0 in her university psychology program while strung out. However, Cara's inner turmoil became too great to handle with the demands of school.

Cara dropped out and spiraled. She fought herself, she fought anorexia, and she tried to avoid the violence of her girlfriend. The police finally arrested her abusive lover, but Cara's weight dropped to 78 pounds. Pneumonia almost killed her as it went septic, and at the age of 27, she was arrested for trafficking heroin and meth. In that low place, in the misery of detoxing in jail, God met Cara where she was. The Bible came to life as she read it in the loneliness of her cell.

Rather than giving her a long sentence, the court ordered her into the program at The Ranch. Miracle after miracle took place inside Cara as she surrendered to Christ. God broke spiritual chains and healed her in ways she'd never expected.

She finally began to eat and gained much needed weight. Cara eventually met and married a Christian man, and God did the ultimate miracle on her broken body and gave her a baby, something the doctors had said was impossible. Cara had given up and was ready to die, but God came to her rescue and gave her an abundant new life.

Because that's what God does. Satan is a liar and a thief, but

Jesus Christ is the King who crushes Satan's plans. Satan seeks to destroy God's children, but God hands them gifts of mercy and healing. As Jesus said in John 10:10:

> *The thief cometh not, but for to steal, and to kill, and to destroy: I am come that they might have life, and that they might have it more abundantly.*

These were the stories Tim and his family watched develop month after month, year after year.

"People asked, how did we know that's what God wanted us to do? How could we hear the voice of the Lord?" Tim thought it was pretty easy; it was wrong for him not to help those people.

Plenty of well-meaning folks worried for them. "You're bringing these people into your home? Your kids could get hurt!" The four Remington children might have been molested or manipulated. The recovering addicts went out into the world, to their jobs and families; they could have returned to their mentor home with alcohol or drugs. Tim and Cindy committed their children to the Lord, and He faithfully kept them all safe.

"God absolutely protected my family through the years," Tim readily tells people. God did it. He protected them all.

In the meanwhile, God didn't leave the Remingtons or Beares to do the work alone; He sent other mature Christians to the Silver Valley to help them.

Cindy remembered those days. "There were an amazing number people back in the little parentheses of time who came to our church. They came from different places of the country! Wonderful, spirit-filled, on-fire, God-loving, Jesus-serving people were sent there, I think, just to be a light in a dark place. They had never heard of the Silver Valley, but God told them to go there. So many of those testimonies. It was exciting, because we knew that the Lord was bringing down the darkness, bringing light in and dispelling all those shadows. It was pretty dark for awhile, that's for sure."

Six-and-a-half years after they'd started the Cataldo church, Kelly Cook approached Tim. Kelly's husband Jim had been on the board for awhile, and out of the blue, Kelly handed Tim a piece of paper that said, "Six months to this day, you're going to be full time."

Tim had earned his living by hanging drywall all those years. He'd never wanted to get paid for pastoring. He'd found that pastors who worked day jobs seemed more passionate than those who were paid to do the Lord's work, and Tim didn't want his calling as a pastor turned into an office job, a 9 to 5 routine. He didn't want to be a pastor who stopped getting out there, who expected hurting people to come to him. He worked as a minister, but he paid his bills hanging drywall.

Tim thanked Kelly, but he didn't make much of her piece of paper. He stuck it in his desk and forgot about it. Folks had given Tim supposed words from God on multiple occasions, but those words often came to nothing.

"We're supposed to stone the ones whose prophecies don't come true," somebody teased Tim about this.

"Right?" Tim said. "We could have stoned a lot of people in our lives, but this girl… I didn't think about it twice." Even with a growing congregation, the church didn't have a ton of money coming in. A lot of people were out of work, and it didn't make sense to trust his income to a bunch of recovering drug addicts. It was a scary idea to give up his day job and have the church pay his bills.

Then, it happened. One day, head deacon Randy Seaton approached Tim and told him the church wanted to hire him full time. The idea did not excite Tim. In the end, he agreed to become the full-time pastor if (and only if) the church voted unanimously for it.

"You go to the congregation. You tell them what you're going to pay me and everything. I don't even want to know what it is. If they vote a hundred percent, I'll do it."

Tim only agreed because he knew there were a couple of old

Floods and Drugs

church ladies who didn't like him, and he felt certain they'd vote against the proposal. That night Tim and Cindy went out into the hall, and the church voted. Soon, Randy Seaton came out and said, "It's a yea." The church had voted unanimously.

Tim approached one of the older ladies who didn't like him, a blunt woman named Delilah, and he straight up asked her why she had voted for him. She grimaced. "I don't know!" Delilah later became a good friend, the sort who always said exactly what she thought. Tim chuckled, "When she was mad at you, she was mad at you."

An orchestra of personalities and ragged backgrounds filled that church, and God tenderly worked in them all.

That night after the vote, Tim went into his home office and opened the secretary's desk to find that scrap of paper Kelly Cook had handed him. He held up the note and examined it, and sure enough, six months had passed. To the day. The Lord had nailed it right to the day. Tim called up Kelly and said, "You're not going to believe this-"

"Why?" Kelly said. "Why wouldn't I believe it?"

With that, Tim started pastoring full-time for Cataldo Lighthouse Ministries. Working all day as a pastor gave Tim more time to do counseling and work with people one-on-one, and he loved it. He was able to go out any time of day and meet people in their homes.

Tim thought back over the many people God had saved through the ministry. There were multitudes of great stories, broken people who were healed, who became pastors and ministers themselves. Including The Altar's church secretary, Adella.

14
Adella

A spunky woman with rich brown eyes greeted visitors to The Altar church every day, directing them to the appropriate offices, scheduling appointments, coordinating events, organizing the food bank, and helping network all those involved in different outreach programs. She talked to the family members of those in the Good Samaritan program and prayed with people who stopped in for prayer.

"Hi!" Adella said cheerfully. "You want something to drink? Coffee? A Zipfizz?"

"A Zipfizz? What's a Zipfizz?" somebody asked.

Adella gasped. "You've never had a Zipfizz!" She disappeared and returned with a cup of pink, effervescent liquid.

Day after day, Adella served a stream of people with kindness and grace. Day after day, she cheerily assisted visitors who never guessed the crushing destruction of her past. The body and soul of a scabby meth head had been replaced by a lovely, brown-eyed cup of human Zipfizz.

Adella's experiences with sex started early in life. Multiple people molested her from age six onward, and the abuse psychologically wounded her and gave her insomnia. As a child, she didn't understand; she assumed it was all normal. At age 12, she thought nothing of having an 18-year-old boyfriend. At 14, she began smoking meth, and drugs owned the next two decades of her life.

Adella described her life story plainly, but her calm surface hid an ocean of once-anguish. She rubbed her right forearm as she related those years, massaging old tensions out through her muscles.

"I gave birth to my first child at 16 and had my first abortion at age 18." In total, Adella believed she'd had four abortions. "My sister seems to think five, but I remember four. I gave one baby up for adoption, and I had three children that lived with me. Kayla was born in 1997, Madison in 2004, and Joseph in 2007." Kayla now had a beautiful baby of her own, and Adella proudly displayed pictures of the little man on her phone.

While growing up in Puyallup, Washington, Adella made friends with her neighbor Lucas. She and Lucas got together when she was 18 and stuck together through 13 years. They produced little Madison and Joseph, but they were always using, coexisting amidst their drugs and violence.

"I was a crazy meth addict," Adella said earnestly. "We got into physical fights, my family members and I. Our home always looked fine on the outside, but it was crazy inside. My parents had their alcoholism, and I was a meth user. They thought they weren't so bad, because they were only drinking and I was on drugs, but I was manic and we'd get into huge fights."

Eventually the whole family moved from Puyallup to North Idaho, but their troubles just moved right along with them.

Adella survived year after year as she balanced motherhood with work and addiction. "Just as we have seasons with the Lord, we can have seasons in that other world." At times she'd focus at being a good mom. She smoked meth as her drug of choice, but she was able to hold down a job. Sometimes she stayed home with her children, and sometimes she went off partying, leaving her babies and returning home at 4:00 am.

"With Madison, I used meth the first and second trimester, and the last trimester I cleaned up a little bit. I did quit meth with Joseph, but that's when I got addicted to hydros. I went in to get my teeth fixed, and they gave me hydros and I got hooked."

Hydrocodone, oxycodone, and morphine now owned Adella - on top of the methamphetamines - and she put her system through that chemical destruction for years. She didn't know what it was like to not be on drugs; she'd been using the whole of her post-childhood life.

While telling this part of her life, Adella continued to rub her left hand up and down her right arm as though her arm were in pain. Her face remained calm, but the anxiety bulged up in her. "I can only talk about the abortions now because it's been years," she confessed. "It was something I kept secret. It was like a car accident in my heart. When I first told Deborah at The Ranch, I was literally shaking because I couldn't believe I was saying the words. I didn't speak about it to anybody, ever."

Those abortions crushed her. "It was very traumatizing. I blocked some of them out. A friend told me when she had hers, she was out for two weeks, like a complete blackout. And I'm not really an emotional person. It was rough, that time in my life."

None of it completely destroyed her, though, until the day that 15-year-old Kayla came home with some emotional news - news that Adella has chosen to keep private from the world.

"I'll never forget that moment, because I thought, 'Oh my goodness, what do I tell her?' I had been through it all, and I didn't know what to tell her to do." They lived in a split level house. After the conversation with her daughter, Adella left Kayla down in their basement room and slowly stepped up the stairs.

"Mind, body, and soul, I just lost it. Here, my sins were repeating in my daughter. You always want what's better, what's best for your kids. And I knew Kayla's struggles were because of my life, my craziness. That's when something totally broke in me. I remember it so perfectly. I walked up the stairs, and it was like slow motion. I went to the back sliding glass door and opened it to go out to smoke a cigarette and look at the sky. That moment, I completely fragmented."

By Memorial Day weekend, her sister had become so worried about her, she convinced Adella to check into the hospital. Adella was a manic, suicidal mess when she went in, but she came out even worse. The hospital gave her prescription drugs to help her get off a long list of narcotics, but she only lasted three days. Because she had checked herself in, she could also check herself out, and they couldn't keep her.

Adella's brother Jacob wasn't any better than she was. They were a mess together.

During that time, self-condemnation and shame overwhelmed Adella. Her body started to cave in under the devastating emotional weight, like the woman in the Bible who was bound over from her infirmities:

And, behold, there was a woman which had a spirit of infirmity eighteen years, and was bowed together, and could in no wise lift up herself.

Luke 13:11

The shame and guilt and unforgiveness in Adella's life had bound her over, and no matter what she did, she couldn't lift herself up. Even in those seasons when she looked like she was doing better, she wasn't. She had been trying to handle it all in her own strength, and she couldn't do it anymore.

Adella quoted Luke, "But, the Lord said to that woman, 'Woman, you are loosed from your infirmities,' And immediately she was made straight."

To be made straight herself, Adella had to first fall completely flat. Her grandmother had given Adella the power of attorney over her estate, and of course Adella blew through her grandmother's money.

"Talk about more guilt. Just keep piling it on. Pile it on." Adella shook her head.

After wasting her grandmother's estate, Adella broke into

her parents' house to look for things to sell. She had worked all her life, but now she couldn't hold it together enough to keep a job. Her mother accused her, so disappointed, "Adella, you were never a thief." That's when her parents finally said, "We're done with you. Don't come around."

In September, Adella had no money, no way to get high, and she could feel herself coming down. She couldn't handle it. She couldn't face life sober. She couldn't face the overwhelming shame of all the things she'd done. She and Lucas had separated, but she had no money to move out. Lucas lived upstairs while she and her brother Jacob slept down in the basement room, because they had nowhere else to go.

On September 25, 2012, Adella got into a fight with Lucas, a fight that ended up changing her life. Lucas had said he'd give her $20 but changed his mind and told her he wasn't giving her any money. Adella completely flipped out.

"I wanted to die. I had a vision of myself slicing up my wrists. I was crazy. My family, my kids, they never knew what they were going to get with me. I weighed 90 pounds; I was all teeth and eyes. Complete bones. So, Lucas and I got into a big fight upstairs. Then, Jacob came upstairs and shoved me and said, 'Stop acting like such a junkie!'"

Enraged, Adella screamed, "A junkie calling me a junkie? I'll show you. My blood is going to be on your hands! I'm done with this life!" The vengeance rushed up in her. If she killed herself, they would all have to deal with it! "My brother was a strong guy, and I was only 90 pounds, but when you're so demonically oppressed and so angry... I had an incredible amount of strength."

Jacob grabbed her and tried to put her in a choke hold, but Adella fought and wrestled with him until they were spitting in each other faces. Lucas didn't stick around. He grabbed the two younger children and left so they didn't have to watch their mother and uncle batter each other in the living room.

Adella finally broke free and ran downstairs to their basement room. She locked the door and looked for something sharp, something she could use to cut herself and bleed to death. The mirror. She took up a crutch to break the glass of her big mirror, banging it twice without success before Jacob broke in and grabbed the crutch. He threw her onto the bed and shoved his forearm against her neck.

"We're better than this!" he shouted. "We're better than this!"

Physically weak and emotionally broken on the bed, tears oozed from Adella's eyes. "You might be better than this," she choked. "But, I'm not."

In that moment, all the disgusting things she'd said and done rushed into her mind, and she thought, "I'm a loser. I'm a loser! And I'm always going to be a loser. I don't know how to be a mom. I've wrecked my children's lives. Madison is seven-years-old, and I'm telling her that I won't always be around for her. I've failed my older daughter. And my son, he's just the cutest little boy, and I'm his everything, and I'm always behind locked doors where he can't come. What kind of life is this? I have no purpose in my life!"

Jacob took the chair and stood at the end of the bed, and they both cried together. Then, they heard a, "Boom boom boom!" on the door.

Jacob said, "It's the police."

"Go hide," Adella whispered, because Jacob had a couple of warrants.

The police opened the door into the basement room and walked Adella back up the stairs. Bruises over her skinny, scabby body told them of the physical battle she'd waged. As she climbed upward, step by step, Adella saw the filth of her home: dirty kids' handprints, stains on the carpet, holes in the walls. She walked into the living room and noticed the trash, so much trash. Dishes piled up. Clothes everywhere. Knives on the floor. Adella gazed around and saw her whole life as garbage.

One officer asked, "So, what's going on? What's going on

here?"

"I'm a mess," Adella said. "I'm a mess. There's something wrong with me."

The other officer appeared upstairs after a cursory search through the basement. "It's clear." He hadn't found Jacob.

Adella must have visibly relaxed, because the officer returned down the stairs to hunt again. After a minute, she heard Jacob's voice bounce up the stairs. "Hahah... you found me!"

A voice spoke in the back of her mind as Adella slumped on the couch, "This is the way it has to be. This is how it has to be." Adella tried to get up to go to Jacob, but her officer stopped her. "You can't go down there."

"That's my brother. My brother's here. That's my brother!"

The officer downstairs had handcuffed Jacob, but in kindness he said, "You can come down and give him a hug." Adella rushed to see Jacob before they took him off to jail.

"Adella, I'm going to be okay," Jacob said as she hugged him. "This is the way it has to be."

She stopped. That's exactly what she'd been thinking.

He told her, "I'm going to get help. You need to get help. And I love you."

Adella trudged back up the stairs, so defeated. The officers regarded her with mercy. "We can take you to the hospital."

"No!" she said. "Please. Please don't send me back there. I don't want to go back there."

"Well, then your other choice is jail," the officer warned her.

"Wait! Wait, there's a pastor. Pastor Tim. Lucas has the number." Lucas had worked with somebody who went to Tim's church.

"Who is Lucas?"

Thank God Lucas had gotten the kids out, because he was able to avoid arrest and stay home to take care of the children. If Lucas had gone to jail, the kids would have been parceled out to foster care. Adella called Lucas at his parents' house, and he returned home and called Pastor Tim.

Meanwhile, dogs snuffled down the hallway, looking for drugs. Of course, Adella and Jacob had used every bit of every drug in the house, so the dogs found nothing. Adella thought, "Wow. If they sniff up anything, I'll be so upset, because all of this will have been for nothing." The whole eruption took place because she'd faced the agony of withdrawal.

Lucas' phone call worked. Soon, a pastor walked into the living room wearing a vibrant floral Hawaiian shirt. Pastor Tim. Embarrassed about the mess, Adella moved clothes off the couch to make a place for him to sit. Tim ignored all of it - the trash, the dirt, the bruises - and asked her, "So. What is your purpose in life?"

Adella looked at him and thought, "What? Do you see this house? What? Purpose to die? What are you talking about?"

"Where was God in this?"

God?

Adella knew God. She did know Him. She didn't know Jesus, but she understood that God existed. Her grandmother had served as secretary at the Catholic Church, and even though Adella had been the wild child, her mom sent her off to all kinds of churches when she was young.

Many years after that 25th of September, Adella thought back through her life and recognized that God had intervened when she'd sought Him. "When I was a little girl and I'd been molested, I had insomnia. Really bad insomnia. I remember getting on the floor, crying out to God, crying like a baby. 'Please,' I begged. 'I just want to sleep. I just want to sleep.' I put my hand up, and it felt like Jesus was right there." Adella didn't know He was Jesus, but she felt Him, and she fell asleep in peace that night.

"When Pastor Tim asked me about God, I thought, 'What God? Look at my life!' I mean, God was out in the universe, and He didn't care about me, and I didn't care about myself."

The pastor studied her and asked, "Do you have any finances for the program?" He glanced over at Lucas.

Adella said, "I don't know. We'll work it out."

Adella

Then Tim looked at her as though he knew her, and he had so much mercy. He said, "Okay, get your stuff and we'll go."

Adella tried to collect some clothes. She had sores all over - on her belly, on her arms. At The Ranch they called them her "picks" because she had picked at herself as an addict on meth. At this point, she wandered around her living room in a daze, trying to find something to take with her. "Are these clean? Is this clean?"

She collected a few things, and Tim drove her to the church for her intake. Cindy and Gracie and Jadon walked in, and they all took Adella to Denny's to eat and talk. Tim asked Adella if she'd ever heard of The Ranch. She hadn't. He tried to give her a description of the program and what to expect when she got there.

An hour later in the car, Tim said, "I know you're going to be dancing for the Lord. I can just see you loving Jesus." Then Tim said, "I can't believe you've never heard of us. We go to the jails. We help people-"

"You go to the jails?" Adella interrupted in excitement.

"Yes."

"My brother! My brother is in jail. They took him."

Tim grabbed a random envelope and a pen. "What's his name? Write his number down."

"Jacob! Jacob Eckstein." Maybe they could help Jacob too!

Tim and Cindy took Adella into the woman's home at The Ranch and introduced her to Deborah, one of the mentors. Adella had become so weak, spiritually and emotionally and physically, she hardly stayed awake the next several days. She smelled like filth to herself. Nausea and sickness overwhelmed her as she came down from the drugs, but the staff took care of her. As she entered the bathroom at The Ranch, she saw a plaque above the toilet, the exact same plaque that her sister had in her house quoting a portion of Jeremiah 29:11: "*I know the plans I have for you, sayeth the Lord.*"

"The program at The Ranch is regimented," Adella said. "But I really needed that. I needed that routine." Days passed as she suffered through detox. Deborah came into the bathroom to help her up from where she lay on the floor, and Adella wailed, "I want to go home now. I know now what not to do. I want to go home. I want out. I promise promise promise I'll be okay!" It was the sickness talking, the unwillingness to push through.

Deborah faced her, full of intensity and fire. "You're not going anywhere. You will die out there!" She gently helped Adella get into the tub.

"And all this dirt and filth came up," Adella said. "I looked down at myself in the tub, and I saw my white, skeleton body. So thin. So weak. That's when I finally said to God, 'Okay, you can have me.'"

She had never read the Bible in her life when she started at The Ranch, and it was hard to understand at first. As the ladies read it every day, though, it started to come to life. One day, Adella read John 16:21:

A woman when she is in travail hath sorrow, because her hour is come: but as soon as she is delivered of the child, she remembereth no more the anguish, for joy that a man is born into the world.

That verse struck Adella right in the chest, and it helped her get through detox. Adella was a mother, the mother of children living and dead, and this was something she understood. She was in travail, she was in sorrow, but her new life was the joyful birth to come.

The ladies in her group read Proverbs every day, and as Adella went through each week, memories started coming back. Her sister had given her life to the Lord, and they would get into big arguments because Adella had been a scoffer for so many years, her mouth filled with cursing and bitterness. Her mom had even said, "Get of out of my house. I can't understand you!" Adella thought about the person she'd been, all the things she'd said, the oppression she'd been under. By the time she reached The Ranch, she had plain died inside. There was nothing left of her. She wondered if she really had died, and she was in a sort of spiritual school after death where she'd better get it right or she'd go to hell.

One day during dinner, Deborah said, "We got Jacob!" Pastor Tim had been visiting him in jail, and Adella's brother was accepted into the program. "But, he's not coming today. He'll be coming November 25th."

Adella counted the days on the calendar, and she realized that if Jacob came in on November 25th, they'd graduate the same day. The women's program lasted four months, but the men's program only took two months.

On January 27th, 2013, Adella and Jacob graduated from the program together. They were the only two to graduate that Sunday. On September 25th, they had been fighting, spitting and wrestling, and on January 27th, they both stood on stage at the church and celebrated together.

"It's all been a spiritual dance. I've learned to dance in my walk with the Lord. I love to worship Him in dance. I can't believe what He's done in my life, and I think about my testimony all the time. I don't want to forget. I think we forget about the miracles that God has done in us. I don't say I didn't backslide here and there, because I totally did, and God picked me back up, and we kept going. That's another story for another time, but He saved my life."

Adella's salvation led to the salvation of her family members. Kayla's life improved and by the time Tim was shot, she was doing well and living with Adella. "Kayla is amazing. I've got a grandbaby now. That's why… God has totally redeemed my past to good now. Does that make sense? He redeems the time. He does that. What Satan meant for evil, God has made for good. I depart from what is evil. I seek peace and I pursue it."

Madison and Joseph lived with their father, but Adella had a good working relationship with Lucas and saw the kids a lot. Jacob and Adella had to walk out their new faith when they got out of the program, but their parents saw it and also gave their lives to the Lord. Their other sister had long believed in Jesus, but she was freed from alcoholism along with their parents.

"Now, they're all following the Lord, and they're not drunks anymore. Everybody is doing well, and they all work in the ministry. It's so amazing. I'm so content," Adella smiled. "Sometimes I'm reminded of the old pain from all of it, but I trust the Lord in my life. I trust Him. For the Lord has plans. He has plans."

On March 6, 2016, Adella got a call to return to the church to show law enforcement security video of Pastor Tim's shooting. She walked through the dark building to the back, where a single light shone from Pastor Tim's office filled with waiting officers. Surrounded by all those people, Adella logged in and found the footage. At that moment, nobody knew if Tim would make it, and Adella had to watch Kyle Odom stand and fire at her friend, the man who had so gently led her from her filthy living room - her filthy world. She had to watch her pastor slam into his car and drop to the ground. Grief overwhelmed her as she replayed the terrible scene, even as hospital staff down the road labored to replace the pints of blood that had poured across the pavement.

Through the horror, a new thought entered Adella's head. "Wait. The dreams. He told me over and over about his dreams. In the dreams, he lived."

Justine. Angel. Adella. There was another important church leader whose story needed to be told. Kyle Odom had planned to kill another man that day in March: Pastor John Padula.

15

JOHNNY

Kyle Odom shot Tim Remington, but his plans had been to shoot John Padula too. Johnny. The church leaders all called him "Johnny," and he gave warm hugs like a good big brother. Hurting people knew they were safe when Johnny Padula came around.

In 2005, the Remingtons started working to build a physical church in Cataldo. They had outgrown the Canyon school, and they really needed a bigger building. They tried and tried to push through the red tape to construct a church in the Silver Valley, but it became too much. It made sense to start a church in Coeur d'Alene, and so Cataldo Lighthouse Ministries eventually bought a building on Best Avenue, back on the other side of the Fourth of July Pass. They named their new church The Altar, and Johnny Padula eventually came to serve as the outreach pastor there.

For Christmas in 2017 and again in 2018, Johnny dressed like a homeless man and sat on the sidewalk in front of Ross Dress For Less in Coeur d'Alene. He settled down and waited for people to give him money, but he stopped the folks who tried. Instead of taking anything from them, he handed them a card with cash and scripture verses in it.

"We want to bless you instead," he surprised them. "God bless you. Merry Christmas."

A young lady walked out of the store on a day near Christmas, a child asleep on her shoulder. When she approached to give him a few bucks, John said, "That's not what we're doing. We want to bless you today." He handed her a card, and she thanked him and walked off. Minutes passed, and the young woman returned, tears in her eyes. She said, "That card blessed me so much. A year ago today was my mom's service. My mom passed away, and the Lord spoke to me by what was written in that card. It's what my mom used to say to me all the time."

This author once worked with that young lady; her mother and two older brothers had both died. Within a few months, she'd lose her father as well. A little verse in John's card reminded her that she wasn't left alone; God still loved her and was looking after her.

KHQ TV and the *Coeur d'Alene Press* sent reporters to watch John and record as he greeted people and gave them cards, and they didn't edit away his Christian message. They showed John praying with people in the name of Jesus. The whole purpose of going out dressed like a homeless man was to bless people and remind them of God's love for them, and Johnny Padula had a lot of fun doing it.

In 2016, John texted Bible verses to 399 people every day. One of the girls in the program had changed her number but hadn't updated John, and future shooter Kyle Odom randomly received her old number when he moved back to Idaho after leaving Baylor University. In his disturbed state, Kyle interpreted John's group texts as coded messages from the government. John quickly realized that Kyle wasn't the young lady who'd previously owned the number, so he called and told Kyle about his own life and how Jesus had saved him. Then, John invited Kyle to church.

John never met Kyle personally. Kyle didn't come the weekend John expected, and when he showed up on March 6th with his .45 caliber handgun, John was gone preaching at another church. If John had been there that first Sunday in March, Kyle might have hammered him with holes too. Tim alone faced Kyle Odom on his warpath to kill the aliens, because Johnny was out of town.

John has never claimed to hail from Mars. In fact, he came to know the Lord from a pit of darkness as deep as any other human. He had his own story; God had rescued him several times before

Johnny

he ever risked death from Kyle Odom.

John grew up in Kingston, Idaho, raised by two caring parents on the west side of the Silver Valley. For no apparent reason, a rage constantly churned inside John. All his emotions, all his intensity funneled into rebellion and anger.

"It was my sin nature, and anger was my thing. I was angry all the time. I'd smash stuff and chase my sister with hammers."

John was kicked out of the Kellogg School District in the 5th grade. He repeatedly lost his temper and fought the other boys until the school finally told him not to come back. His parents had to move to Coeur d'Alene to get him into another school, but he got kicked out twice more by the 7th grade.

His parents divorced during this time, and John moved to Las Vegas with his dad for more than a year. He tried to go back to school, but after three days someone pulled a gun on him, and that ended his school career. Instead of history and math and English, John got into gangs and drugs, and his life deteriorated from there.

For the next 17 years, John spent his days high on crystal meth. He turned to pornography in all its forms and slept with any girl who came along. He was that guy. When he moved back to Idaho, a seven-year stay in prison forced him to get clean, but John immediately started cooking meth again when he got out in 2006.

Meth gave John energy. It made him feel good. "Speed. Going a hundred miles an hour. Had all the energy in the world. Wanted to accomplish everything."

Then, John met a girl who went through the rehab program at The Ranch, a girl he actually cared about. He'd never before worried about pleasing a woman; he used women like he used cigarettes. They'd always been tools, there one day and gone the next, and he'd long lost count of the multitudes of females who went through his nights. This one, though. He actually cared about this one. She was going through the Good Samaritan program, and she kept trying to get John to go through it too. He was desperate to hold onto her, so he listened.

Cindy remembered those days. "Johnny would come in, skinny

with bad teeth. He'd sit in the back of the church, slumped down in his hoodie, his head shrouded by his hood. He was there only because he was waiting to see her."

John finally agreed to go into the program. "I ended up going in for a day or two, then I left. I was strung out on meth. I was 137 pounds and my teeth were all broken out."

He tried the men's version of The Ranch for a few days before he took off. His girl wouldn't let up on him, though. She repeatedly said, "You need to go back to rehab or it's over between us." He paid attention.

John tried it for a few more days, then left again. The final time, he stayed long enough for the men to share the Gospel with him, and John agreed to accept Christ as his Lord and Savior. That changed everything. "I was absolutely born again," John said.

John hadn't realized that God was alive and well and willing to change his life. He thought that God was some old dude thousands of years old and maybe dead, and people went to church to celebrate Him. He had no clue God had created all things and exercised power over the whole universe. He didn't realize that God could look into his own life and make it brand new.

One night during his third try at The Ranch, a man named Chris Anderson prayed over John, and God gave Johnny Padula a brand new life. Chris was a gnarly looking guy with tattoos all over his bald skull, but willing to do anything to please the Lord. This tough, weathered man prayed for John, and God heard him.

"I didn't have to do anything. All I did was shut my eyes when Chris prayed for me. When he put his hand on my shoulder, I wanted to punch him in his mouth because I was so full of darkness, and I didn't understand the whole darkness and light thing. I was instantly... I just closed my eyes and, as he prayed, man, I started weeping for my sin. I didn't even know what sin was, but I started weeping."

John didn't feel condemned. He felt the conviction of the Holy Spirit, and by the time Chris finished praying, tears rolled down John's face. "I opened my eyes. It was in the driveway of The

Johnny

Ranch, and it was like I could see the green of the trees." A sob caught in Pastor John's throat as he related that precious moment. "And I could see that the sky was blue. And I had never noticed those things before." The tears of conviction turned to laughter in the driveway as joy, real joy, filled John's heart.

Ten years later, Pastor John looked like the neighborhood dad, somebody who should be out throwing a football with the kids. A trimmed beard warmed his full, healthy face, and he still had most of his hair. His eyes held gentle humor. There was nothing harsh about his demeanor, nothing hard. He looked like everyone's big brother, a comfortable and trustworthy man, compassionate and good. He talked about dogs and hiking in the woods. He prayed with people about their troubles or gave strangers cards with scriptures and money for Christmas. The skinny, angry man in the hood had vanished.

The full transformation took time, but John was different after Chris prayed for him. He still couldn't relax and be calm in one place, and John once again abandoned the drug treatment program. Still, he'd changed. He went by his friends' houses and threw away their drugs in an effort to help free them too. He had completely lost his desire to use, and he became a passionate, annoying evangelist telling all his friends how they had to get saved.

"Yeah. I didn't know how to minister to people. So, I was taking all their stuff, and I was like, 'Come with me,' and I'd take them to meet the pastor. Then I'd sit there until the pastor walked out, and then I'd say, 'Hey! This is my friend so-and-so, can you minister to him?' Finally, Pastor Tim said, '*You* can minister to them.'"

John didn't know how to do that. "I should have stayed at the rehab. I would have learned the Word of God a little bit and understood that stuff."

Giving the Lord control over his life had made the difference in John. The anger vanished – that rage that had hounded him since childhood. His foul mouth dried up, and he no longer cursed with every other word. His serious pornography addiction dropped away, and he didn't even think about it.

John stayed with that same girl for another three months, but all the while he returned to the bars and strip clubs and all his haunts to talk to people. He prayed over his old friends and explained the Gospel and told his story about how Jesus had saved him. His girlfriend didn't like it, though. She didn't think it was a good idea to frequent strip clubs and bars and the houses of his old drug buddies.

"It looks bad. You're not above reproach."

John didn't even know what that meant! He wouldn't stop going to all his old hangouts to share the Gospel, because he wanted those people to get saved too!

Finally she said, "I'm done," and she left him. For the first time in two decades, John Padula felt his emotions. All the years since he dropped out of school, he'd stuffed away his heart or numbed it with drugs, and he'd never learned to deal with natural, healthy, normal feelings. He didn't know how to experience anger or pain or sadness or rejection. He felt happiness for the first time when Christ came into his life, but that emotion was much easier to handle than this new awful sense of loss and grief. For the first time since Chris Anderson prayed for him, John got high.

Of course, that allowed addiction's foot to jam back into his life, and he couldn't get the door closed again.

"I kept coming to meet with Pastor and coming to church services, and I'd cry at the altar and beg God to take it from me, then I'd leave and get high. Finally, one Sunday, I stopped by and brought Pastor Tim and Al Gregory some coffee before church. I was strung out, but I popped in to say 'Hi.' When I was leaving, I put my head on the steering wheel and said, 'Lord, You have to stop this. I can't stop.'"

As he told this part of the story, tears welled in John's eyes again. "I left and went to the house where I was staying. When I left, I saw a K-9 unit. And as I was driving, I said, 'This is it.'"

The cop searched John's car and arrested him. He was

sentenced to 16 days in jail, but that was the best thing that could have happened to him. While sitting in jail those days in 2009, he repented and started reading the Bible. John had been going around and talking to all his friends in excitement over what God had done for him, but he had no scriptural foundation. He'd left The Ranch before he'd learned what the Bible actually said. Those days in jail, he had plenty of time to get into the Word of God, and he no longer had a drug problem when they released him. He began reading the Bible on a regular basis, and that helped him continue to walk with God for the rest of his life.

Pastor John kept pictures of his old self on his phone, skinny and bald with bad teeth, but The Altar's outreach pastor no longer resembled the meth head in his pictures. A powerful metamorphosis had taken place in John since 2009. Even between two of John's mugshots, a hint at his change shone through. In the first mug shot, a thin, bald guy looked coldly at the camera.

"That was before I came to Christ."

In the second shot, the same guy gave a toothy smile - entertaining since he was on his way to jail. "And that's after I

Figure 15.1 - John Padula's conversion displayed in two mug shots.
Left: hardened John before salvation. Right: joyful John after Christ saved him.
Courtesy John Padula.

got saved and walked away for those three months."

After that, John had victory over all his old addictions for the rest of his life. "No drugs. No porn. No alcohol."

Of course, learning to walk day by day with Christ took time. It was a process. Pastor John explained, "The first couple of years, emotionally, it was up and down. I'm super emotionally driven, and I didn't have emotions my whole life, because of the drugs and the anger. So, learning to feel appropriately and know that… hey, it's okay to cry. It's okay to be sad. It's okay to be happy. It's okay to feel these emotions God gave you, as long as they don't rock your faith." At least he didn't go slugging people in the face anymore.

God had so much mercy on John, over and over, in many different areas of his life. His sins were not held against him, not even the damage caused by his sins.

For instance, his lifetime of drug use had destroyed John's teeth, but God didn't abandon him to the consequences of his actions.

"I prayed for about a year, because I was just embarrassed. I sold insulation door-to-door, and I love people, so I was always talking, but I was covering my mouth all the time. I prayed for about a year that the Lord would allow me to have new teeth. I shared my story with Sinai Family Dentistry, and at first they said, 'Yeah, we don't do anything like that,' because I had no money and no insurance. They called me back three days later and said, 'Hey, the doctor wants to see you.' They put me in a study club with all these people and studied my mouth for a while. These oral surgeons, all these people, they all donated everything to fix my mouth. Like, 25 grand. Fixed my whole mouth."

Pastor Johnny smiled, a full smile with no brokenness, no missing members among his pearly whites.

"Yeah, it's crazy. The Lord's provision for our lives. Not that we deserved new teeth, because we ruined them. He gave us ones to begin with, and we ruined them."

God also allowed John's felonies to be purged from the system.

Johnny

Tim travelled with John down to Boise in April of 2019 and went before the parole commission. John had become a pastor reaching into the lives of other troubled people, and the state recognized his obvious change in life and his brand new lease on the future. They pardoned all of his felonies. John got his rights back - his gun rights, his voting rights. Everything.

Of the many blessings, one of the greatest, was when John met Amanda. She went through the program in 2009, and they were married in 2011.

It didn't take long for both John and Amanda to go into ministry. As a brand new married couple, they had people detoxing on the floor of their tiny apartment. They bought a house where they developed an overnight discipleship fellowship for recovering women. In 2015, they switched to a men's house, offering a stable transition to those who had graduated from the program.

"Right now I have six guys that live in my house. We've had that the whole time. We have the six month outpatient program, where we have four or five different options for people who don't have good housing. And one of them is our house. So, we've had hundreds of people live with us."

John and Amanda enjoyed it, and the men didn't cause any serious problems. There were occasional personality differences between the guys, and some were better at keeping things clean than others. Even if the men got frustrated with each other, there were never issues with fighting or real trouble. John charged a small amount for rent, because the whole idea was to help the men learn to be responsible, but he didn't charge much. They were working to save up money so they could get their own places and move out into the world.

God gave John freedom from his old addictions. He gave him new health and new teeth. He gave him a wife, and ultimately, God gave John children.

All those years before he was saved, John slept with hundreds and hundreds of different women, and he never produced a child. He might have had dozens of little Johnnys out in the world, but none of his liaisons produced a baby. While in prison the first time, John went into the doctor for a related problem, and they told him he couldn't reproduce. The drugs had taken their toll on his body, and he couldn't have kids. God took John's broken, mangled life and gave him a brand new one, and a decade after their marriage, John and Amanda had four healthy children together, four children in a house with recovering drug addicts.

Johnny shrugged. "My kids fall in love with all of them, and they're all like family with my kids."

The God of the universe took a foul, angry, messy human being and made him a pillar of blessing and mercy. John proved a source of stability and brotherhood to hundreds of men, but he also became a faithful friend to the author of this book. He's the sort of person one can call up at odd hours and say, "I'm in a serious situation! Please pray for me!"

That's what God does, though. He takes people who are suffocating in manure and grows them into flowering plants that produce His fruits of love and kindness. In exchange for destruction, He gives them beauty. He gives them life.

That's the biggest and most important miracle in the world - the miracle that Kyle Odom could never have blown away

Figure 15.2 - Pastor John Padula, courtesy The Altar Church.

16
PLAYING PIANO

We don't live five minutes at a time. We live second-by-second. In the hospital, Tim had literally counted thousands of seconds, "678, 679, 680, 681, 682, 683..." Those seconds were important to him. As they passed by, each meant one more second of life, one more moment of pressing through.

Before Tim left the hospital that first time, several doctors stood around his bed and said, "See if you can move your right hand." They all stared at his lifeless limb. It lay there like a cold, dead fish as he concentrated and tried to make something wiggle. His right ring finger twitched the tiniest bit, and everybody shouted with excitement. That single twitch meant a smidgen of life existed in his nerves, and where there's life, there's hope.

For months, Tim's right arm was cradled in a sling, completely useless. They smothered it in ice every night to numb it enough for him to sink away into sleep, but he couldn't move it at all. Even after the shattered bone healed, the nerves couldn't fire to each other right. Connections had been destroyed. The nerves constantly called out, but the messages couldn't get through, and the result was never-ending misery in Tim's forearm. He agreed to take a little pain medication but not nearly as much as the doctors recommended. He couldn't do a blocker for the pain for long, and he didn't want to be drugged out. He learned to deal with the pain by disassociation, by separating his conscious mind from the constant suffering in his hand. He might sit and drink a milkshake and talk like a normal person, but he'd unconsciously rub his arm up and down, up and down – just like Adella had done when dredging up the deepest miseries of her past.

Cindy did what she could to help, taking time to massage Tim's muscles or make him stretch and unstretch his fingers. Specialists came into the Remington home, and every effort was made, but nothing fully worked to soothe the constant agony.

They prayed. The whole church prayed for Tim's arm, taking shifts fasting and interceding so that somebody constantly sought Tim's healing every hour of every day. For a whole year the church prayed, day after day after day. The pain continued.

Three years later, Tim walked almost normally. The hole through his pelvis and damage to his shoulder still bothered him, and if he pushed himself too hard, the ache bent him over. Seven years later, the damaged wires from Tim's right shoulder to his hand continued to spark and burn. We don't live life in years, though. We live life in seconds. Moment by moment, Tim pushed through one day after another day after another.

"If you had told him that his hand was going to hurt like that?" For four years? Seven years? Ten years? Cindy shook her head. "He wouldn't have been able to handle it."

Even then, God did miracles with Tim's damaged brachial plexus. Normally, people injured in that bundle of nerves want their arms removed because of the vicious, relentless burning involved with the nerve damage. Tim? Tim wanted to play the piano again. Tim loved the piano. It was his favorite form of worship, his time of seeking God's peace and comfort after a crazy day at the office. Tim served hurting people as a critical counselor, and he spent all day talking people through suicidal thoughts and guilt over rapes and murders. After a long, draining day, the piano offered Tim a way to decompress and spend time relaxing in God's presence.

About nine months after the shooting, Tim asked a neurologist if he'd ever be able to play the piano again. The doctor shook her

Playing Piano

head and gave Tim a smile. "Don't even hope for that. That isn't ever going to happen. Don't even hope that it will ever happen, because it's never going to happen." Like a horse kick in the chest.

Of course, Tim went home and started trying to play the piano.

People who knew him understood how important the piano was to Tim. It was physically impossible for him to do it, but several people decided to pray specifically for that one thing, that God would allow him to play again.

He still couldn't feel the fingers in his right hand, but he started working those fingers and working them, and slowly, excruciatingly, he learned to press down the piano keys. The left hand had to dominate, but as weeks and months passed, Tim increasingly managed to stumble through songs with the fingers of both hands.

Tim didn't complain about any of it. He had to go about his days, doing his best to get back to the work God had for him. It was Cindy who remarked about her husband's struggles in the post-shooting world.

"Here's the thing that I've personally come to. The Lord miraculously preserved Tim's life and kept him from crazy things. The fact that those bullets missed his vital organs is just crazy. The one that pierced his jacket but not his shirt? That would have certainly been a death shot, because it would have hit his heart. The Lord stopped that bullet. What the Lord did not allow, He did not allow on purpose. So, we have to also know that what He did allow, He allowed on purpose. It's not like He said, 'Oh, whoops. One slipped by.' He didn't drop the ball. We don't know what the reasons are, but there are an awful lot of people who have been affected by the very fact that Tim is in pain, and yet he keeps on."

That's a sober truth. A woman who suffers through childbirth knows that her pain ends when the baby is born. Even the ceaseless grief of a deep toothache can be halted by removing the tooth. Tim had no relief for his burning hand year after year, day after day, second after second. The thought of it should mortify any feeling person.

Cindy agreed. "I hate it for him. I'm grateful for everything the Lord is doing, and I trust Him completely, but there are some days it's just so hard to watch him go through what he goes through. And nobody understands it, because he presents very well. About twice a year he has a day when he says, 'I don't know if I want to do this. I'm gonna do it, but the idea of having this pain keep on for the rest of my life?"

Tim and Cindy both asked, "What if it isn't better by this time next year? What if by next year we're still doing the same thing?"

The answer is always the same. "Then the Lord will give us grace this time next year."

The first year, Tim thought if he pushed through and pushed through, the pain would eventually go away. And it didn't. After the second year, he had some real discouragement. He had to hope that it would ease one day, or his reality became too unbearable. And through his own suffering, he still, every day, had to sit down with an abusive alcoholic or a guy who'd molested his own granddaughter and continue to minister to them.

The pain did move down. Little by little, it descended down Tim's forearm so that less of it broiled. The whole hand wasn't freed, but there was hope in the fact that less of his arm burned as time plodded on.

Losing his worship time at the piano grieved Tim terribly. He worked and worked, and he forced his right fingers to push down the keys. He succeeded where the neurologist had promised only disappointment, but it wasn't worship anymore. His decompression time, his time of relaxing with God had been stolen from him, and playing piano became labor. He had to watch his fingers now. He had to set each finger down where he knew it needed to be. He no longer had the freedom to close his eyes and lose himself in the music; he had to concentrate and wade through awful moment after awful moment.

Tim started playing on Sunday mornings during the church worship service before giving it all over to another worship leader.

He might perform one or two songs, but he couldn't handle more than that. Then, one day an older man came to church, a man living out of his truck. This fellow grabbed Tim as he walked by and began to rub Tim's arm. A little strange. Then the man told Tim, "When it starts really hurting, the Lord wants you to press through. Just press through."

The next service, Tim played a song, and it got to the point he couldn't do it anymore, but he remembered what the man had said. So, he kept going. For the first time, he closed his eyes and played, and it was like he could see the piano in his mind with his eyes closed. Since that day, Tim has been able to play for most of the worship service, a gift from the Lord who loves him.

According to Tim's neurologist, that was never supposed to happen, but God isn't limited by "never supposed to."

17
KETTLE DRILLING

Doug Kettle should be mentioned at this point, because it's time for more words of encouragement. Tim's forearm burned non-stop day and night, week after month after year, but life isn't merely about pushing through despite suffering. That's not the only story to tell. When a little boy gave his fish and loaves 2000 years ago, God provided abundant food – baskets and baskets more than 5,000 hungry people needed to get full. He gave Justine a purpose and ministry that touched a multitude of lives. He gave John Padula teeth and children he hadn't earned. God is absolutely willing to pour out mercies.

Most people struggle along in their day-to-day lives, working paycheck to paycheck, burdened by the cares of paying bills and getting kids to do their homework and eat their vegetables and get off their phones. We don't see a constant stream of miracles through our days, and we don't expect them. Doug Kettle was no different than any of us.

Doug married his wife Brenda in 1980, and between the two of them they produced eight children to clothe and feed and keep out of trouble. They moved into Kellogg, Idaho from Washington for the simple reason that they needed a house for their multitude, and it was hard to find anybody willing to rent to a family with eight kids. Little guys spill drinks on the carpet and carve their names in walls; few landlords wanted to risk the destruction imminent in a house of young folks. Doug and Brenda had struggled unsuccessfully to find a place in the Tri-Cities of Washington, but when Doug looked in Shoshone County? He found a house for his family within half an hour. The Silver Valley proved a good place for Doug and Brenda, not just because of housing, but because the silver mines up and down the valley offered plenty of contracting jobs for Doug's drilling company.

As a young man, Doug had a talent for drilling, but nobody wanted to listen to a 20-something kid or give him any real responsibility. To bypass all that and get respect, Doug lied about his age. He even acquired a fake ID that aged him. He hung out with manly men, tough dirt and sweat miners, and he spent a lot of time in the bars. Doug managed to keep the bills paid and food on the table, but he developed a real drinking problem.

Soon after they moved, one of Brenda's friends invited her to Cataldo, to a church in the Canyon school. Brenda dragged her husband with her, and Doug liked Pastor Tim Remington, but he wasn't a big church-goer. Doug had gone to church as a kid and knew the truth about God, but it wasn't Doug's thing and he skipped a lot. It wasn't so easy to escape, though, because Tim didn't stay inside the church doors.

"He chased me down!" Doug said. "He wouldn't leave me alone!"

It was a good thing, too, because Doug's drinking had become a serious problem and a threat to his marriage. "I was only able to stop drinking for six or eight hours at a time," Doug remembered. His marriage had tumbled to the verge of a divorce when Tim convinced Doug to enter rehab down at Calvary Ranch in California. The trip saved Doug's marriage, his liver, and his life.

When Doug went down, he looked gray. During that month, life returned to his face and mind and his whole body. His addiction had been replaced with a fire for serving Christ, and the internal changes pushed right out through his skin, altering even his physical appearance. The gray alcoholic Doug had converted into a healthy, full-of-life Doug. Brenda flew down to attend Doug's graduation, and when he met her at the airport, she walked right past him because she didn't recognize him.

Doug said, "They broke all the rules and let me go rent a car to pick her up at the airport. I stood at the end of the gate when she got off, and she walked past me. I said, 'Brenda,' but she didn't stop. She kept walking around the corner. I had to follow her. 'Brenda,'' I said. 'Brenda!'"

Doug had changed *that* drastically, inside and out. "They took a picture of me when I got to the Ranch and another when I left, and I think they still have those two pictures up on the wall to this day."

Doug's rehab graduation took place on February 14th, 1996. St. Valentine's Day. Instead of getting divorced, he and Brenda took that day to renew their vows, and they celebrated 40 years of marriage in 2020.

Doug's business had been eking along, and he lived from paycheck to paycheck like everybody else in the Silver Valley. One particular week, he and Brenda had to make the decision about whether they were going to pay their rent or pay their tithes. They prayed about it, and they decided to trust God and pay their tithes.

"God did so many things, so many things. This was one of the early miracles He did for us."

On Monday, Doug loaded some antiquated junk heads onto his trailer to take to the scrap yard to recycle. He'd finished packing up the trailer when some guy called him from Salt Lake City asking if he had certain parts - the parts that happened to be those very hunks of metal that he'd just loaded onto the trailer. The guy was willing to pay $10,000 for those old heads, and that astonished Doug. He'd trusted God, and God dumped $10,000 into his hands.

This is not the health and wealth gospel. Doug was not paying God "seed money." God had some important jobs for Doug to do, and when Doug trusted God, the Lord gave him the funds to do those jobs. Doug had started his drilling company so his wife could stay home and raise their eight kids, but after Doug gave His life to the Lord, God started doing huge miracles in that drilling business.

First, though. First, Doug had to go around to all his business associates and make things right. He'd been lying for years – lying about his age, lying about his accomplishments.

Tim said, "He was the kind of guy who would sit down with a fellow at the bar and talk about Vietnam. They'd swap stories, and they'd cry together. But, Doug had never been to Vietnam." Doug had the whole biker persona going on. He'd wanted people to think he was bigger and badder than he was, and he'd spent his whole life trying to impress people.

Doug realized that he had to come clean to everybody, but he worried that honesty might destroy his business. He wanted to get bigger drilling contracts, and he didn't have a lot of capital. He needed all his suppliers to front him the supplies, and if they knew what a liar he'd been, they might just tell him to take off. Frankly, Doug was trying to do something crazy. Folks don't normally start a big drilling company unless they have a half million dollar drill and another million dollars in the bank, and Doug had nothing. No big companies were going to give him contracts, because they didn't know if he had the funds to buy gas for his machinery. A drilling company needs cash set aside to buy parts, to fix its drills if they break down. Doug had a $16,000 drill, he needed $60,000 in drill rods alone, and he needed all his suppliers to miraculously front him the materials in order to move forward.

It was a crazy venture, but Tim and Doug prayed about it, and Doug decided to go to all his business contacts and tell them the truth. He had to. As part of his new life in Christ, he had to start by being honest with everybody. One-by-one, Doug and Tim travelled to businesses around North Idaho.

"I was there," Tim said. "I watched each one of them as he gave his testimony. I watched their faces as they listened to him, and they all shook their heads and said, 'Right on.' Then, they gave him everything." With his $16,000 drill, Doug started to get contracts with some of the biggest mining companies in the world.

Doug said, "The Lord allowed me to get that drilling company going for nothing, and I really believe he did that so that I could bless other people."

Not long after, Doug flew down to Phoenix to buy a flatbed truck. He only wanted the service truck, but the fellow at the truck dealership kept bugging Doug to look at a drill.

"The government is auctioning off this drill. You should go look at it."

"I don't need a drill!" Doug insisted. "I just need the service truck."

The guy wouldn't leave him alone about it, so Doug finally agreed to at least check it out. The government had bought a half-million dollar drill, but it was the wrong model for the state's needs, and it had only about 60 hours on it. Doug looked at it and realized that he knew it. He had worked for the company that built the drill. He couldn't use it for the jobs he had, but he knew what it was worth, and he scraped together every penny he had, broke his piggy bank, and bought that drill at auction for $25,000. He could sell it for ten times as much.

God had even better plans. As soon as Doug got home two days later, he found an Echo Bay Mining bid request on his desk for a job in Russia, and they needed the specific drill he'd just bought! Echo Bay not only paid Doug $250,000 for use of the drill, they paid him $180,000 just to transport it to Seattle. He knew all the tooling it needed, and Echo Bay put up the money for everything he ordered. What's more, he got paid a 20% commission on the tooling. They paid him to ship the drill out to Russia, and they paid him the contract for doing the drilling. When the drill came back to the U.S., it was spraying oil. He put a brand new motor in it, but the oil problem was fixed by replacing the oil sending unit – a small, inexpensive part. After the contract ended, Doug sold the drill again for $200,000.

That drill jump-started Doug's business, and he became a millionaire. He doesn't like to talk about it, because wealth hadn't been his goal. God blessed his company, plain and simple, and because God blessed Kettle Drilling, Doug was able to bless other people. He paid cash for the first men's facility when Tim wanted to start a home for men. He held the loan, with only Tim's word that Good Samaritan Rehab would pay him back.

"If he couldn't pay it back, though, that would have been fine. I had it in my heart to give it to him," Doug said.

That was the purpose of it all. Doug had a talent for drilling. He was good at it, and he loved to do it. God poured out His blessings on Doug's company and Doug has since been able to come to the aid of others in need.

"Tim is for the downtrodden," Doug said with emotion. "The amazing thing about Tim is that he doesn't get hung up in the results. If you fall off the wagon and trip and land in the dust, he doesn't stress out. He's all about the things that God can do through you. He's a very special anointed man."

What if Tim hadn't chased Doug down, hadn't kept bugging him, hadn't taken the time to convince him to go into rehab down at Calvary Ranch? What if Tim had simply minded his own business the way most people do? Doug might have drunk himself to death, leaving Brenda to raise eight children on her own, adding them to the statistics of the destitute.

Doug sees miracles all throughout his life. God had been chasing him long before Tim got into the mix, but the successes in Doug's life are a direct result of Tim's faithfulness to obey God's leading. First Tim obeyed God, and then Doug followed suit, and God was able to take that obedience and multiply it into blessings for all kinds of people. That's how God works. We trust Him. We stay faithful to the small things He asks us to do, we give Him our little fish and loaves, and He does the rest.

18
Radishes and Cherries

Here's a puzzle, a question for the ages:

Is God's will always done?

We need to answer this question well. People assume God always gets His way, that all things happen the way they do because He wants it. "God has His purposes," they say mysteriously when some tragedy takes place, and it often sounds flippant rather than comforting. Even then, are they right to blame God? When Adella was molested as a little girl, was that God's will? What a horrible idea! Did God want Johnny to use all those women like disposable garbage? No! No. Did God tell Kyle Odom to shoot Tim? Certainly not.

Jesus told us to pray, "Thy will be done." If God's will were done, the fruits of the Spirit would reign wherever we looked. Love, joy, peace, patience, kindness, goodness, gentleness, and self-control. Those are the things God loves. Those things are God's will, and God's will is *not* always done on Earth as it is in Heaven right now.

God hates sin. He hates it. His laws order us to be good to one another, but the whole world has rebelled against Him. What's more, He's going to punish all acts of evil one day. The great Judge of the universe will mete out a long withheld justice, and that's a terrifying prospect. We all want to be under His protection and not His wrath in that day. Either our sins are paid for by Jesus' death, or we pay for them, but somebody has to pay for our disobedience.

We live in a corrupt, fallen world doomed for destruction, and we only enjoy our freedom because God is patient. God is longsuffering. God is willing to wait for the John Padulas of this world to leave their angry, selfish lives behind and give themselves over to His healing salvation. Thank God for His longsuffering patience, else we'd all be destroyed. But, there is something especially remarkable that God does, something exceptional that has blown away those like Justine and Adella and Johnny - those snatched away from the jaws of death. When they gave God their broken, messy, empty lives, He turned all those broken pieces into blazing beacons of light.

Sin causes destruction, but when we trust and obey God, He gives us beauty for our ashes. It's those who trust in Christ who can take courage in the truth of what Paul says in Romans 8:28:

And we know that all things work together for good to them that love God, to them who are the called according to his purpose.

Jesus Christ never said His followers' lives would become easier by following Him. Jesus warned His disciples over and over that persecution and struggles awaited them, and during the Last Supper, Jesus told them they would have many troubles. But he said, "*Be of good cheer; I have overcome the world,*" (John 16:33).

Trust. That's what they learned, those He saved. They learned that if they trusted God and obeyed Him, He did wonderful things despite their troubles and even through their troubles.

Sometimes, though. Sometimes God allows things that just don't make sense to us, and we are asked to trust Him even then. "Even if it feels like gravel in our mouths," Cindy said one day. "Even if it's not the outcome we wanted." Cindy lived with Tim's

Radishes and Cherries

pain day after day, year after year, having to trust God even while she watched him suffer with no earthly end in sight.

Jesus never treated people flippantly. He intimately cared about their suffering, and we're told in Romans 12:15 to weep with those who weep. When He allows things in our lives that cause us to weep, though, He asks us to trust Him through all of it.

Sometimes life can be like Doug Kettle's, and blessing after blessing washes over us. Sometimes we push on and on like dear Tim in endless pain. Every life wades through seasons of both blessing and agony, and Jesus reminds us, "Be of good cheer. I have overcome the world."

Cindy said, "Remember Lazarus." Lazarus. Jesus' close companion, who died because Jesus delayed His coming.

Jesus often stayed with Lazarus and his sisters when He travelled through Bethany, and Lazarus was Jesus' personal friend. Lazarus mattered to Jesus. John 11 tells us Lazarus' sisters sent word to Jesus to let Him know his friend was sick, and Jesus told everybody that the sickness wouldn't end in death. Then, Jesus waited another two days before He set out to their home! He intentionally waited and arrived only after Lazarus had already passed away.

This delay caused a temporary faith crisis in Lazarus' sister Mary, who loved Jesus. Mary had given her heart and soul to the Lord's teachings, and when she needed Him to come heal her brother, He failed her. That's what it seemed like. He said the sickness wouldn't end in death, but then He didn't show up until it was too late. Jesus hadn't healed Lazarus, and it's Martha and not Mary who goes out to meet Jesus on the outskirts of town.

"It's Mary of Bethany not wanting to see Jesus because He dropped the ball," Cindy said. "She couldn't bear to look at Him. She thought He loved her, and she had expected Him to come running to heal her brother, and He didn't." Before the Lord even walked into town, Martha went out to meet Him, but Mary stayed back in the house. Cindy felt Mary's wounded disappointment. "She'd been sitting at His feet, hanging on His every word, totally in love with this wonderful person. She thought He loved her, but then He didn't heal Lazarus, and it made her think 'He isn't who I thought He was. He didn't love me like I thought He did.'" The death of Lazarus presented a whole paradigm shift for her.

This time around, Martha was the sister of greater faith. When Martha heard that Jesus was on His way, she didn't even wait for Him to arrive. She rushed up the road before He'd reached the village, because she knew that Jesus could do anything. She trusted that He had it all in His hands. She said, "Lord, my brother wouldn't have died if you were here, but I know that God will still give you whatever you ask."

Jesus didn't hold back. He let her know right then that Lazarus would come back to life, telling her in the next verse that her brother would rise again. Martha misunderstood what Jesus meant, and she expressed faith that Lazarus would resurrect at the last day. She trusted Lazarus would have eternal life, and she thought that was the most important thing, but Jesus took her another step upward. Not only did Jesus have the power to heal people, it was He who had power over life. That's what He needed to make clear, what He had to show the world. They needed to know who He was. Jesus told her in John 11:25-26:

> *I am the resurrection, and the life: He that believeth in me, though he were dead, yet shall he live: And whoever liveth and believeth in me shall never die. Believeth thou this?*

Martha did believe it. She believed that He was the Messiah, the Son of God.

After this revealing moment, Jesus sent Martha to quietly get Mary. Mary, who had remained in the house.

As soon as Jesus called for her, Mary rushed to Him in her great heaviness of heart, and she fell down at His feet sobbing, saying, "Lord, if You had been here, my brother wouldn't have died!"

If You had just been here! If You had just come when I asked, He would still be alive! The heartbreak in her voice bursts from the page. She pours out confusion and crushing disappointment, distraught that her beloved Jesus would have abandoned her like that.

This leads to one of the famous verses in the Bible. John 11:35 states simply, "*Jesus wept.*" Jesus started to sob too.

"It's not because Lazarus was dead," Cindy said. "It's because their grief grieved Him."

Jesus knew He would raise Lazarus from the dead, just as He knows He will raise all of us one day, but He still felt Mary's deep sorrow. Jesus had a purpose in letting Lazarus die; He has purposes in everything He allows, but pain always matters to Him. He sees it, and He feels it with us. We are not abandoned children. We're not alone.

Not so long after this, Mary would pour expensive ointment on Jesus' feet in worship, but in that moment of pain she felt devastated. She couldn't see past the moment. She didn't understand that what the Lord had in mind was better than what she'd ever hoped.

It's so easy to feel like Mary. The greater picture is vast and beyond human sight, and it's easy to feel dropped and unimportant in the bigger work God is doing. It's easy to feel like God doesn't see and doesn't care. If His children could just sit with Him for a bit, each and every one of them would see how deeply important they are. Even those things that Satan means for destruction, the evil that God rejects and hates, God can redeem those things and turn them over to good when His children hand their lives over to Him.

One day all the hurt will be over. God will hold us in His arms and comfort us in real, personal ways - face to face. Isaiah 25:8 says that the Lord will swallow up death in victory, and God Himself will wipe the tears from our faces.

"We go to God and we beg and plead and cry for Him to accomplish our plans," Cindy said. "Which is okay if we also beg and plead and cry for the grace to accomplish His plan, to actually go to Him with the same urgency and fervency, with a desire, 'Please help me to do what You want me to do.'" When God moves, it's like a train that nobody can stop, and we want to pray for the very things that He has in His heart to accomplish. There are things that we know He wants done. He wants people to be saved, snatched from the jaws of death. He wants His kingdom to come. He wants us to live in freedom, rejoicing in His goodness.

God had not healed Tim's broken nerve connections, and Tim had to - had to - put his life completely into the Lord's will every day. Tim knew God heard his prayers, his desires, large and small, and yet God had chosen to leave Tim suffering for a time. Not forever - for a time. "But, what I've found," Cindy said, "is that God works in the delays."

The Lord made promises to Isaiah that didn't come to pass for 700 years, until after Jesus was born. Sarah waited 25 years for a baby, and she caused problems by jumping the gun, trying to make it happen before God's timing. Just because God is biding His time doesn't mean He's not working behind the scenes in the meanwhile.

Cindy smiled. "I love Galatians 6:9:"

And let us not be weary in well doing: for in due season we shall reap, if we faint not.

Cindy elaborated on what she meant, "Due season means, if you plant radishes, you're going to have them in a few weeks. If you plant cherry trees, you'll have them in a few years. Due season is when it's time, and only the Lord knows the best time."

Cindy recalled one woman in particular who was frustrated because she kept being delayed in starting treatment at The Ranch. She was able to be with her mom during that time, and then her mom died. The young woman moved into The Ranch after her mother's death, into a safe place. If she'd been out and about after her mom died, she might have jumped off a cliff. God's timing was so perfect, He had her there at the perfect time for what she needed in her life. If certain things happen too soon, then people

Radishes and Cherries

are vulnerable and at risk, and if those things happen too late, the people reap unhealthy crops. God's timing is just right.

Jesus did love Mary and Martha and Lazarus. He loved them so much. When they sent word to Him, He came. And He didn't come too late; He arrived at exactly the right time. It wasn't simply about Lazarus' not dying; it was about showing the greatness of God's power. It was about showing that Jesus was Himself the Resurrection and the Life, to show that He had the very power to raise a dead man.

Jesus felt her pain and bawled with Mary over the death of her brother. Then, still full of heaviness, He walked over to the cave where they'd buried Lazarus. He prayed, and then He called Lazarus alive from the dead. The Lord's plans were so much greater than the sisters had realized, and all the while that Mary felt abandoned, it turned out she hadn't been dropped for a moment.

Jesus told us in Luke 12:7 that every one of our hairs are numbered. We are the riches of the universe. When we approach God with the cries of our heart, He sees us. He knows.

19
PASTOR TIM GOES TO BOISE

For we wrestle not against flesh and blood, but against principalities, against powers, against the rulers of the darkness of this world, against spiritual wickedness in high places.

Ephesians 6:12

Tim had done a great deal of work in the counties of North Idaho, but in January of 2020, God sent Tim south to the seat of the Idaho government in Boise. Tim never campaigned or worried about an election, but God slipped him into the Idaho state legislature at a particularly significant time in history.

District 2 state representative John Green was indicted (and later convicted) for tax evasion and conspiracy to defraud the United States, and the ethics community told him to step down. The local Republican Party had to present possible replacements to the governor, and they chose Pastor Tim Remington. Governor Brad Little nominated Tim, who officially took Green's place on January 28th. Tim finished out Green's term, serving until December 1, 2020.

January 28, 2020. Widespread concerns over a new strain

of coronavirus had already been sprinkling through the U.S. population as people became aware of deaths in China. Seven weeks later, President Trump shuttered the economy for fifteen days to "flatten the curve" and Covid-19 interrupted life for the next two years. Tim's term in the Idaho state legislature began at the end of January. "Right at the onslaught of disaster. Which is why I believe I was there," Tim said. "I told the Governor that I wanted to go down there to unify our party in Idaho, because it's very fractured."

Tim flew to Boise as the 70th state representative, and he found the body muddled and chaotic in its makeup. He immediately set to reading the bills that came across his desk, but he learned that few other representatives did this. He read every single bill he ever voted on – all the way through – but plenty of other state reps voted on bills they'd never read! (It's exhausting work, and honest and decent lawmakers should introduce short, to-the-point legislation.)

Tim finally decided that about 12 of his fellow legislators were thoroughly dedicated, solid people who could be depended on to support conservative values, and a few others had potential. Over the course of his year in office, Tim found that too many of his fellow lawmakers – far too many – were just politicians. Even if they passed solid bills, they were simply playing the game.

Heavy issues were moving through the state legislature in early 2020. One of the first bills Tim encountered during that legislative session was the Fairness in Women's Sports Act (HB 500), introduced by Barbara Ehardt (33A). The bill made national news by seeking to ban biologically male athletes from women's sports. Due to the promotion of transgenderism during the Obama Administration, biological men who identified as female were entering women's sporting events in different locations across the country and beating all the biological women. Ehardt sought to protect women's sports by outlawing the practice in the state of Idaho. She told the *East Idaho News*:

Boys and men will not be able to take the place of girls and women in sports because it's not fair. We cannot physically compete against boys and men. The inherent biological, scientific advantages that boys and men have over girls and women, even if they were to take hormones, even if they were to spend a couple of years on estrogen, that's not going to replace the inherent biological advantages that boys and men have.[1]

Three different bills came up on transgender athletics during Tim's 10 months in the legislature. Governor Little signed Barb Ehardt's bill HB 500 on March 30th along with HB 509, which prevents transgender individuals from changing their genders on their birth certificates. Those bills easily passed both the House and Senate, and the governor signed them.

There was less consensus, however, on how to handle Covid-19. Brad Little and Tim Remington butted heads over the 2020 business closures, especially when it came to keeping people out of churches.

All the states shut down in March to get ahead of the Covid-19 pandemic. The whole country went into quarantine. Businesses closed. Students remained home from school. Churches shut their doors. On March 26th, Governor Little ordered Idahoans to remain home for 21 days with the exception of certain "essential" services like grocery stores, liquor stores, and veterinarians. Churches were regarded as nonessential.

Tim and the staff at The Altar did not regard their church as nonessential. "We have drug addicts and people on the verge of suicide and people escaping violence coming in here. We are absolutely essential!" The Altar kept its doors open, and Tim received angry letters from all around Coeur d'Alene, even from Christians, criticizing him for endangering people in the middle of an epidemic.

---

1 Mike Price, "Ehardt to Introduce Bill Banning Transgender Women from Women's Sports," *East Idaho News*, January 20, 2020. https://www.eastidahonews.com/2020/01/ehardt-to-introduce-bill-banning-transgender-women-from-womens-sports/

In the end, Tim bit the hand that fed him. He sued Governor Little in order to prevent another shutdown of churches.

"I did not want to do that. I helped Brad Little get appointed, and he knew that. It didn't feel good to sue him at all. I loved the guy. I really felt for him, because I felt like he was a pawn in this whole thing. But, I also knew we had to fight him on his own turf." Tim spent a lot of time praying and talking to his fellow legislators. "I knew that if I did not sue him right away, he would have locked down the churches again. Our lawsuit was the only thing that kept him from making the churches nonessential."

Governor Little hit back. Tim introduced Bill 340 regarding rules for juvenile facilities in Idaho. He wanted to open a juvenile home, a Good Samaritan drug rehabilitation facility for minors, and his bill passed in both the House and Senate. Governor Little vetoed it. "Because I was suing him for taking our freedoms," Tim said. "I learned a lesson; you sue the governor a little bit after you need your bill signed."

When Tim returned home as a full time pastor, he had greater appreciation for the many forces battling over Idaho's state government. On the final day in April after *sine die*, the legislators were all leaving to return to their home districts, and Barbara Ehardt encouraged the representatives to come together so that Pastor Tim could pray for everybody. Of the 70 lawmakers, 23 gathered in a back room for prayer. In Idaho - Republican, conservative Idaho - just one-third of the state representatives could be bothered to join Tim's prayer.

In Daniel 10, Daniel fasts and prays to God, and after three weeks an angel arrives. He explains that he was sent as soon as Daniel's prayer began. He was sent immediately, but the angel encountered spiritual opposition and spent 21 days battling past the "prince of Persia." Three weeks he battled, until Michael the Archangel, the prince over Israel, arrived to help him. The angel gives Daniel his message then explains he has to go back and continue to fight the prince of Persia and then the prince of Greece. These were angelic battles going on outside the view of Daniel's physical eyes, and the angel's story gives us an interesting picture regarding the affairs of government.

Daniel 10 suggests that there are spiritual forces over countries, spiritual forces that may be for or against the God of the universe, which raises a clear question about the "prince of the United States." What spiritual forces battle over America? Since its foundation, America has claimed the God of the Bible as its God. The United States' national motto is, "In God We Trust," and its Pledge of Allegiance declares it as "one nation under God." Does a righteous angel like Michael preside over America, or have evil forces raised their flags over a country whose God is no longer the LORD? What does it say about a country when the majority of lawmakers in even the most conservative states won't take a few minutes to pray?

It mattered that Governor Brad Little vetoed Tim's bill, that he blocked Tim's efforts to create a juvenile version of The Ranch. Real teenagers out there needed help escaping drug and alcohol addictions. Real lives were at stake. It mattered whether biological men were permitted to compete in women's sports, or whether churches were able to remain open to serve people during a pandemic. The laws passed by the lawmakers had effects on normal, everyday people on the ground. They had real-life consequences.

Tim found some good folks wrestling in the Idaho government, working to pass laws that protected the people. However, there were plenty of politicians in it for their personal reasons, politicians who didn't necessarily have the best interests of the people at heart. Regardless of the number of "D"s or "R"s behind the names of those in office, it became clear to Tim how vital it was that Christians prayed regularly for their state officials. The governor, the House and Senate, the judges all needed prayer, and the people of Idaho had the responsibility of conscientiously voting and holding up their political leaders. If godly men and women didn't take their places in government, that meant the laws would be made by people who didn't fear God, and America desperately needed God's blessing.

God's arm is not short to save, but we need to seek His face. If we want the spiritual powers over America to be holy ones, we need to call on the Lord for His help. We surrender to Him, and He does the hard stuff. As God told Solomon:

> *If my people, which are called by my name, shall humble themselves, and pray, and seek my face, and turn from their wicked ways; then will I hear from heaven, and will forgive their sin, and will heal their land.*
>
> 2 Chronicles 7:14

"My people." It's not on our annoying neighbor across the street or the prostitute downtown. That means us. We are the ones called to humble ourselves and pray and turn from our wicked ways, so that God - who is faithful - can heal our land.

20
NOT DESTROYED

"There is a war that's going on. It's a spiritual war. We can call it what we want, but we ultimately need to rely on the power of the Holy Spirit." - Tim Remington

That's the final message. We are in a spiritual war, and we can absolutely win. We can win if we're fighting in the power of God.

The shooting created a lot of serious suffering for Tim Remington, but it also gave him a gift as a pastor. He could stand up in the public courtroom of the world and declare the indisputable fact that God had saved his life. He could describe the things that the enemy wanted to do and make his case boldly to the judges or prosecutors or public defenders of the world. They all had beliefs of their own - their own views of what took place in the spiritual realm outside the sight of our physical eyes. Tim now had the position to offer them additional testimonial evidence. He could give an eyewitness account of what took place, describing from his experiences the reality of demonic enemies and their desires to destroy us. Those evil forces wanted to rob and pollute and kill us, but they were no match for God. Jesus had defeated them.

Tim could speak to these things, and whether they were Christians or not, the people in the world's courtroom had solid and verifiable reasons to listen to him.

It was nothing short of a miracle that Tim Remington survived. Clearly. Obviously. It didn't take a brain surgeon to recognize the crazy fact that Pastor Tim should have died that March day in 2016. He wasn't seated in the back of the plane where the statistics looked best; he'd been shot repeatedly in the torso with .45 hollow points. He'd taken a bullet to the head. Tim won a victory that defied all the probabilities.

The Lord taught Tim a lot through the years. The depravity of humanity isn't just spiritual depravity. It's physical, mental, and social as well. *"Not by might, nor by power, but by My Spirit,"* the Lord said in Zechariah 4:6. After he was shot, Tim couldn't move his finger outside of God's power. He couldn't speak outside of God's guidance. Before he was shot, Tim's mind had worked fast, like a Zipfizz. After the shooting, it took energy to process his thoughts, and he no longer offered fast comebacks. Maybe that was a good thing; he couldn't insult people "flash-bang" anymore.

Tim's true victory extended beyond the physical, though. Through Christ Jesus, he overcame Satan's efforts to crush a flourishing ministry in North Idaho. That was the bigger issue. In his fury, Satan had longed to end Tim Remington, to end John Padula, to cripple a church that offered God's mercy to a trail of broken people. God allowed Kyle Odom to shoot Tim, but He also turned it back around for His glory. He not only thwarted Satan, He set aflame the worst ordeal of Tim's life so that it blazed as Tim's greatest beacon of light. A shining city on a hill cannot be hidden. The bullets that had pierced Tim set on fire and flashed to the world, "God is alive and well, and He loves to rescue us."

People in Idaho were touched by Tim's preaching and counseling, but the whole country was touched by Tim's shooting. News of Kyle Odom's attack stretched across the miles to the state house and even to the White House.

When 19-year-old Tim Remington prayed a simple prayer in an old van at the edge of a cliff, his whole life changed. Because he gave himself wholeheartedly to God, other lives were changed as well. Johnny and Adella, Justine and Angel are not alone. God is ready and able to free any one of us from the messy sewage of our lives, to clean us up and turn us into burning torches for the world. He can save people at Calvary Ranch in California or through Good Samaritan Rehab in North Idaho, or in jail cells or living rooms or Denny's parking lots in other cities and states and countries across the world. He can use anybody He wants for His great purposes.

God is not limited. He takes our decades of ugly and turns them around for good. Like the Deborahs or Chris Andersons at The Ranch, we can be the conduits God uses to pour His forgiveness and healing on the people around us. He can raise us from the dead like Lazarus and make us shine the news that God still moves in powerful ways.

2 Timothy 3:7 warns that some of us are ever learning but never coming to knowledge of truth. If we're never coming to the truth, that means we're never coming to Jesus, because Jesus is the Way, the Truth, and the Life. He is the key. He's the crux of the whole matter, and through Him we can do all things.

What if there had been no Chris Anderson to pray for John? What if Tim had remained hidden safely behind his desk? Who would have been there to help all those people? People whose lives desperately matter? People for whom Jesus poured out His blood?

We live our lives second by second. Second by second, moment by moment.

"Are you with Jesus?" Tim warned, "Look out world. The gift, the miracle that lies within each of us, is the life of Christ in us. You and I, we're not just physical beings anymore. We're not of this world."

To those who struggle.

May you win every battle

in the power and love of Christ Jesus,

King of the Universe.

About the Author

Amy Joy Hess is a research writer and analytical chemist who enjoys paleontology as her bad habit. She has written many hundreds of news digest articles related to the Bible, science, technology, international politics, and current events and has ghostwritten more than 30 books. Additionally, she is the author of a series called Science & Wonders, which follows the movement of God in her life during her time as a university science student. She is passionate about Christ's impact on her own life and the lives of those around her. Amy Joy is married with three biological children, an adopted son, and nine amazing stepchildren.

www.ingramcontent.com/pod-product-compliance
Lightning Source LLC
Chambersburg PA
CBHW022105040426
42451CB00007B/136